Heartbake

Heartbake

A BITTERSWEET MEMOIR

from my heart to yours —
♡ Charlotte

CHARLOTTE REE

ALLEN&UNWIN
SYDNEY·MELBOURNE·AUCKLAND·LONDON

For Mama, my greatest love of all—for knowing
how our hearts and our stories are entwined,
and for trusting me to share them.

contents

This is my life in all its messy, imperfect, delicious glory.

I have written about moments and mouthfuls as I remember experiencing them. Some moments are sanguine and sweet, some moments are sour and bitter. At the heart of my story are those whom I love and those who love me in return. And scattered throughout these pages are memories of people I once loved, who are now lost to me.

This is my story of learning to trust myself and having the courage to begin again.

I am sharing this with you because I believe that words have power: the power to wound, and also the power to heal. Nothing anyone says or does to me could be worse than the things I have said and done to myself. And nobody can take away from me the work that I have done to nourish myself, to come to love and understand myself.

These are my experiences of moments when I was at my most vulnerable, when I craved connection—with friends and with those that I had only just met. And I satiated these cravings by immersing myself in the ritual of cooking and baking for others, and for myself. And in doing so, I came to understand that food too has the power to heal, and to nurture.

And so, I welcome you to my heartbake table. I would love for you to cook and bake my recipes, to share and devour them—in generous portions—with family, friends or, decadently, just with yourself.

I hope that you will savour each and every mouthful.

It is, after all, my whole heart on a plate.

fragile

Let everything happen to you: beauty and terror.
Just keep going. No feeling is final.

RAINER MARIA RILKE,
'GO TO THE LIMITS OF YOUR LONGING'

At its most fundamental, cooking is the process of applying heat to food—baking, boiling, frying, grilling or sautéing. It is heat that changes something into a different thing, transforming it. And so it was with my husband: the warmth of that first touch; the fervour of that first kiss; the intensity of our bodies combined—raw hunger and heat.

From the moment my husband and I came to be, he was the cook, and he shared with me the secrets of food. He showed me how my mouth and tongue would learn to remember flavours, bitter and sweet, sour and spicy—and salty. His hands guided mine to fold and blend and combine till the dry became moist and wet. He presented me with textures, tender and succulent and light, delicious to the taste and touch.

Yet gradually the heat that once transformed me, now began to consume me. I didn't recognise it at first, but I suppose it is hard to tell you are burning when you're already standing in the flames.

I'm not sure how our shared love of food, our shared love of cooking, our shared *love* became a source of resentment, of control. But I know that I am lonely in my marriage. That while I eat, I never feel fulfilled.

In twenty-four hours, I will leave my husband.

In forty-eight hours, Sydney will enter its first lockdown.

form

*Our three basic needs, for food and security and love,
are so mixed and mingled and entwined that we
cannot straightly think of one without the others.*

M.F.K. FISHER, *THE GASTRONOMICAL ME*

I have one framed photo of my mum and me from my childhood. We are at Whian Whian. She is sitting on a step and I am leaning towards her, arms by my side. She is bending forward, cupping my cheeks in her hands, kissing my forehead. This photo is the first thing I would save in a fire.

Mama, Mum, Mother, Mamacita, Mummy. She smells like Opium perfume, smells like home. Her face is cherubic with eyelashes as long as my own. Our voices are so similar that it is hard for people to tell us apart. She rarely brushes her hair and does not wear make-up, she never shaves or plucks. She was always so much more fun, so much more colourful, so much more alive than my friends' mothers. And so much younger, too. My mama is joyful, energetic and generous. She is a strong, independent woman who loves fiercely. Mum breathes you into her when she hugs you. When I see sunflowers and rainbow lorikeets, I think of her. She is a gifted storyteller, and she makes me laugh out loud. She loathes deadlines and rejects schedules. She loves food but a cook she is not. She loves hard gingernut biscuits, Portuguese custard tarts and toasted salad sandwiches. She loves English breakfast tea with a drop of milk. But most of all, my mama adores salt.

Mum tells me of growing up on the beach where she would dive deeply into the salty waves. That, she told me, was where she got her love of salt from. No, not a love—a *need*. She remembers lying wet on the flat beach rocks, and watching as the warmth of the sunshine left lingering trails of sea salt on her skin.

When Mum was twelve, her parents separated, and her world divided. In the years that followed, my mother felt compelled to antagonise and oppose, though no one quite knew why. A psychiatrist told Mum the sense of agitation that shadowed her would soon pass, but instead the shadows became an ensemble of voices in her mind. The psychiatrist told her that medication would quiet their cacophony, so she swallowed the tablets and waited. But instead of a quiet stillness the drugs brought a nervous restlessness in lieu of sleep, and an acute sensitivity to the sun. She became a captive of the shadows—losing what she had once so loved as now the sun only burned.

My mama was still a teenager when my brother was born in 1987. At this time, the neighbourhood priest resolutely refused to baptise the babies of unwed mothers. My nana was convinced that her newborn grandson would exist in a permanent state of Limbo if he wasn't christened. So Nana insisted that my mum invite the priest for morning tea to prove that she was not a jezebel and secure my brother's place at the baptismal font.

The priest arrived early—perhaps hoping to catch Mum off guard—but she was ready and motioned for him to sit on our old salmon-pink lounge. In front of the priest there was a makeshift coffee table. It was set with a tea towel and on top was a cake, which to the knowing looked *exactly* like the vanilla cream sponges sold at the local bakery. Mum explained she had baked it that morning. She moved my brother's bouncinette closer to the priest and went to the kitchen to make tea.

Standing in her 1950s kitchenette, Mum could hear the priest talking to the baby in his Irish lilt. As she waited for the water to boil, she stared at the peeling, orange-flowered wallpaper. In time, Mum would strip that paper and sand the wall, my brother at her feet. She told me that after each sanding, he would look like he'd been coated in fine white breadcrumbs. Years later, after watching a documentary on asbestos, Mum rang my brother to say he'd probably die from mesothelioma.

When the water had boiled, she poured it into mugs, jiggled the teabags, and reached into the fridge for the milk but there was none. She wondered if the priest would see this lack of planning as an innate failure of her mothering. She called out to ask the priest if skim milk would be okay. Yes, he said. Mum lowered her breast over the priest's mug and squeezed her nipple until the tea became a hue of golden brown.

She carried the tea into the lounge room and watched as the priest ate his slice of cake and drank his tea until the mug was empty. And it was thanks to this sweet cup of tea, filled with mothers' milk for the soul, that my brother was baptised, and much to my nana's relief Limbo was averted.

It was 1989 when my mother and father met. He was a student, just finishing his degree. Mum says he had long blond hair tied back in a ponytail, and he wore black skinny jeans, Doc Martens, a long-sleeved tee and a black overcoat. He walked with his hands in his pockets, and in these pockets there was always the book *The Little Prince*, and a small exercise book for making sketches and writing notes. Mum still has the sketches and notes my father gave her; they're quirky and clever and funny. My mama tells me that my father kept a journal, too, just as I do. I have a framed linocut print that my father made of a man seated in the corner of a room, a hand on each thigh. The man looks pensive, almost sad, and he gazes ahead, not noticing the window. Every so often I look at that man and I wonder if my father ever thinks of me.

Mum says she fell in love with my father over his spinach pie with homemade pastry. She never did get the recipe, but her memory of it inspired her to make a version using fillo pastry. This pie was always in the centre of the table at family celebrations, sitting golden in its dedicated dish—square with a matt glaze of blueish grey and handles made from the deep indentations of fingertips in clay. Each of Mum's recipes have their own dish they are served in, and we had found this one together at the Byron Bay markets. Mum had danced her fingertips along the handles and immediately declared that *this* was the dish for her spinach pie.

After two months of dating, my father took Mum home to meet his family: his mother, his father and his brother Jason. At breakfast, Grandma placed a plate on the table piled high with pastries that Mum did not recognise—she had never seen a croissant before and was unsure how to eat one. Papa Ree, my father's father, seemed to sense this, and without a word he began to prepare a croissant, discreetly pausing after each step so that she had time to follow. Papa was like that, kind, and my uncle Jason reminds me so much of him.

In 1991, Mum was seven months pregnant with me, and she was listening to The Sundays' 'Here's Where the Story Ends'. By this time my father had chosen to pursue other romantic endeavours, but a month later, he wrote saying he would like to be present for my birth. Mum declined—a rare moment of modesty. I was born at 11 am on 7 March. My nana was at the delivery and she says that when I crowned, my head was pushed backwards, and part of my eyes could be seen. She says my eyes were open to the world from the start. My father sent a poem, 'The Eyes of Little Charlotte', and Nana says that Mum cried for him.

When we were born, my mama gave my brother and me each our own heart song: a song she would sing to us when we were tired, or sad, or hurt. And sometimes at night I sing it to myself to help me fall asleep: 'Dream a Little Dream of Me'.

In 1994, our family of three was joined by a fourth—the man I call Pa. Pa was quiet and gentle with my brother and me; there was a stillness about him that calmed. When I think of Pa I think of his deep desire for the sea, his collection of longboards, resin fins in red and blue and yellow. His never-ending search for the perfect set of waves, him lying on hot sand. I think of music—Jefferson Airplane, The Who, The Stranglers, Blur, The Rolling Stones, Led Zeppelin, lounge music and Bob Dylan's *Theme Time Radio Hour*. I remember when we would watch repeats of *The Bill*, *Fawlty Towers* and

Monty Python's Flying Circus and we'd all quote the lines in the silliest of voices. Pa loves Scotch, souvenir teaspoons, trains and planes. He loves to sit and read non-fiction books, but he never reads from beginning to end, he only takes bites. When it comes to my mother, he is the epitome of devotion, and you will often hear her telling him how lucky he is to have her.

After school, Pa treated us to custard tarts from Crusty's Bakehouse in Lismore. And when we'd finished the weekly shop at Woolworths in Lismore Shopping Square, he would take us to Wendy's, where my brother got a hot dog and I got a doughnut, steaming hot and rolled in cinnamon sugar. And when the sugarcane harvest had begun, Pa would take us at night to watch the cane burning, the flames dancing and leaping, the air filled with the smell of leaves on a campfire. On weekends, Pa took us on the ferry to Broadwater, to a cafe with its name written in a hedge, letter by letter. We sat under the shade of an old fig tree where we were surrounded by the distinctive saccharine smell of sugarcane. My mum and brother always had the ploughman's lunch and I would have high tea served on a tiered cake stand. I remember eating cucumber sandwiches and little tea cakes from mismatched fine bone china with gold trim and feeling like such a lady.

Pa and Mama had two children each before they met but never had a child together. As my father re-partnered my number of siblings grew by three. There are theories about how birth order affects your personality traits; I, however, am a complicated case study—I was the last born in one family but first in the other. I have read that firstborn children are often diligent and seek to excel at everything they do; they are dependable, overachievers and thrive in a structured environment. The youngest in the family are often outgoing, fun-loving, self-absorbed and attention-seekers. *I am all these things.*

Your family is the source for so much of what forms you: your likes and dislikes in food and music, your passions, interests, hobbies, humour. And, more than that, every family has different ways of being, different ways of knowing; every family has a different love language, expressed in different ways. As a child of two families, you learn one thing quite early on: some families simply do not blend. Instead, they curdle, like milk, into clumps—like my family. The challenge of being from a curdled family is that you spend your formative years trying to adapt to two separate home bases, divided between two systems of loving and learning. I had been formed by my life with Mum, Pa and my brother, where words of love flowed freely. And in this home, along with weekly visits from my grandparents—Nanny, Pop and Grampy—I had a life filled with spontaneous affection, cuddles and hugs and butterfly kisses. For me, this was so different from the life of my father's family, it sometimes made it hard to fit in, even when I so desperately tried to do so.

In my father's family, Grandma and Papa Ree were my one constant. Both had their own way of making me feel like a part of the family. Papa would tell me I looked like my father, and he'd tell me how I was so similar to my grandma. Papa was kind and beautiful. He wore long johns and nightgowns. In the morning, he would tap the bed, a signal that we, his grandchildren, could tumble in and snuggle up next to him. He would read to my cousins and me and tell us stories at night. He gave *the* best back rubs. He was patient and with his gentle words of encouragement I learned how to swallow a tablet when migraines plagued me, just like they did Grandma. Papa was demonstrative in ways that Grandma was not, and I have sometimes wondered if this was the result of her having lost her mother at a very young age. But Grandma had another language with which to show me love and that was food. She would make egg sandwiches and shortbread biscuits. She also showed me how to brew tea leaves in a teapot, and taught me how tea-drinking could be meditative and calming.

Sometimes, after a particularly stressful day, you will find me with my nose deep in the tea caddy, inhaling the earthy, floral, sweet scent of the tea, and somehow I feel instantly calmer.

When I was thirteen, Grandma and Papa took me on my first trip overseas. We visited Paris. I asked Papa if he knew it was called the city of love and he told me yes, he did, and he jokingly reassured me that he would never break my heart. But Papa died just weeks after we returned from our trip, and my heart splintered into tiny pieces.

When I was growing up, there was always plenty of colour. My childhood homes overflowed with an eclectic assemblage of coloured glass and pottery glazed in vibrant hues. My mother, who is soothed by clutter and indifferent to disorder, would confound us all with her need to arrange her collections by colour onto the Ladderax shelving. So now, in my own home, I too diligently arrange my glassware, crockery and books into a spectrum of colours. Coming home after an exhausting day at work, or just sitting with a cup of tea, I love looking at my harmoniously ordered shelves.

Books have been part of my life for as long as I can remember. Even though money was tight, Mum always bought me books, and through their stories I learned about the human conditions of friendship, love, bravery and loneliness. Mum would connect every book to a personal experience of her own or to one of our family's. On the inside cover of one book about growing old and forgetting, she had written in her habitual messy scrawl a short story about my great-grandmother Ollie. A beautiful mother to eleven children, Ollie's mind was lost to Alzheimer's long before we were ready to let her go.

I loved my collection of books, and I knew one day I'd pass them on to my own children, who would read Mum's notes, her snapshots of moments from our lives. But one afternoon I arrived home from school to find that the bookshelves in my bedroom were completely bare. I ran into the lounge room, and in the quietest of voices I whispered what I did not want to be true, 'Someone has taken my books.'

Mum pulled me into a hug and stated very clearly that she had not been able to afford the accumulating fees at my Catholic school, and after some negotiation, the principal and the priest had agreed to accept instead a 'donation' to the school library.

A donation of books. *My* books. *My beautiful books.*

The shock of losing my books back then has led to an almost pathological refusal to part with any book I bring into my home.

Mum and Pa have a wonderful cookbook collection and each visit I manage to snaffle a couple of books and a baking dish or serving bowl to take home with me. But on one visit, I couldn't find the particular cookbooks I was looking for, not anywhere. My anxiety rose as I envisaged a presbytery with a group of priests fawning over the 'donation' of our cookbooks. But Mum insisted that she had not given the books away, that they were downstairs in one of the boxes yet to be unpacked after the move. After the move in 2010, she meant; it was now 2019.

I ventured into the garage and clambered over the sea of discarded delivery boxes to find a stranded pod of removalist cartons. I scanned the labels, but none referred to cookbooks. Then I saw Mum's scrawl—*virgins*—of course, the contents of this packing box would be pristine, cookbooks with pages untouched by my mama's hands. I tore off the duct tape, folded back the flaps, and there were our cookbooks, dozens of them, stacked by colour and just waiting for me to love them.

I love the words of home cooks. Laurie Colwin and Julia Child. Hetty McKinnon and Julia Busuttil Nishimura and Ina Garten. Maggie Beer and Nigella Lawson, too. I often feel that the words flow from the pages of their books until they themselves are in the kitchen cooking beside me, guiding and challenging me. Their cookbooks are intertwined with some of my happiest and saddest memories, of love and of food. The pages, some stuck together, are stained with remnants of sauces, olive oil and wine. Many pages are full of my hand-written notes, and even though I now know countless recipes by heart, I still love to have their books nestled beside me as I cook.

There is one home cookbook that was at the centre of every birthday celebration I ever had as a child and that was *The Australian Women's Weekly Children's Birthday Cake Book.* It is at the heart of one of the sweetest memories I have of my father. He is at my seventh birthday party and has helped to make the Dolly Varden cake—with smarties, not marshmallows. The joy of having my father there made me giggly, and I kept running up to him and saying anything that popped into my head so he would talk to me, engage with me. I would remind everyone that he was my father, and he was *here*. He painted my face and the faces of my friends, and he joked with us, and he was funny. He was *so present* in that moment, and I was so happy.

Over the next few years, my father would fade in and out of my life until, eventually, he chose to fade away completely.

When I was eight years old, I became enamoured with a girl at school called Hannah. She wore neatly ironed uniforms and her lunchbox was always full of homemade treats. On the rare occasion that I was invited over, I'd pretend that Hannah's house was my home. Her house was spotlessly clean and obsessively organised, with everything in its place. Clothes belonged in cupboards, and the bath was for bathing.

At my house, the clothes were in the bath. Everyone's clean clothes were piled in a giant mound of intertwined sleeves and you had to dive into the bath and rummage through it to find your own. In those rare moments when the bath system was challenged by a frustrated garment-seeker, Mum would happily sing: 'The cleaner the house, the angrier the woman'. For my mum, these words were true. She went happily about her day and was never burdened by thoughts of housework.

Mum often sang made-up songs and danced around the house in various stages of undress. Sometimes, she'd seek out my brother and me and pull us into her conga line. Pa, not always so willing, would try to detach on the third run through, but Mum held firm, weaving in and out of the doorways and back through the kitchen, back through the kitchen, back through the kitchen. My brother and I just went with the flow and embraced the familiarity of what we knew—the comfort of chaos and colour.

And from this, my brother emerged to follow our mum's path, becoming a free spirit, a hoarder of metal, copper and tin. I, on the other hand, have recreated Hannah's house, spotlessly clean and obsessively ordered. And the bath, when I am lucky enough to have one, is only for bathing.

For afternoon tea, Hannah's mum would bake muffins and biscuits and from the bakery she would buy sponge cakes slathered in strawberry jam and cream; custard tarts; finger buns with pink icing; crunchy chocolate crackles and cupcakes with hundreds and thousands. After one visit to Hannah's house, I recounted every flavoursome morsel to my mum in excruciating detail. With a scrunched-up nose Mum told me how she hated buns with pink icing, chocolate crackles and cupcakes with hundreds and thousands. But, I reminded her that we *both* loved custard tarts, and muffins too.

When my brother and I returned home from school the following day, Mum greeted us at the door. Her oversized overalls were completely covered in flour. We followed her to the table, and found it set for afternoon tea, with a tablecloth, a teapot snuggled inside a striped knitted tea-cosy, teacups with saucers and souvenir teaspoons. To my delight, Mum then put a baking tray of muffins between us—just like Hannah's mum. We eagerly wolfed them down; they were delicious.

Afterwards, when we were clearing the table, my brother noticed a bulky Woolworths muffin container tucked deep within the garbage bin. He held it up with two fingers, immediately discrediting Mum's cooking prowess and exposing the theatre of the deliberately strewn flour.

But for me it didn't matter that the muffins weren't baked by Mum in our own oven. What mattered was that Mum had listened to my descriptions of afternoon tea at Hannah's house, and had tried to be a mum who baked for me, if only for a day.

Looking back, I realise that this was the first time I noticed the impact food could have on me. How it could transform my mood, make me feel joy. And even today, being presented with any form of baked goods still makes me deliriously happy.

I have never been able to separate food from feeling. All my memories and meaning are embedded in taste and smell. Food has forever been all-consuming, a large part of what defines me. A doctor once told me that the place in our brains that processes smell is close to the limbic system that processes memory. Smell can conjure memories; it is the fastest and most vivid of all the senses. There are few foods that repulse me, but if they do it is because I have a strong memory attached to the smell of them.

At home with Mama and Pa, mayonnaise did not feature in any food offerings, but when I was five it become a traumatic focal point. It was the school holidays, and I was staying with my father and my siblings. My father insisted that I remain at the dining table until I had devoured every mouthful of what felt like a never-ending bowl of mayonnaise-laden potato salad. I sat there long after everyone else had been excused, watching my reflection in the television screen, crying into my bowl. I was both the aggrieved actor and despairing audience in my own potato salad melodrama. My tastebuds have never forgotten, or forgiven, mayonnaise.

When I was four, Mum used my brother and me as guinea pigs to conduct her version of the Stanford marshmallow experiment, which was designed to measure a child's ability to delay gratification. She told us to sit at the dining table, and then showed us our 'rewards'—one plate with a single pink marshmallow and another with three marshmallows. We had a choice, she said. We could eat the single marshmallow immediately, or we could have the three marshmallows if we waited until she returned. Then she left the room.

The moment she had crossed the threshold my brother began scoffing all four of his marshmallows. But I just sat there, looked at the marshmallows on the plates and waited. When Mum returned, she offered me the marshmallows, but I declined; my brother immediately helped himself to my share, so I had no chance to reconsider. But even if I'd had the chance, I wouldn't have taken it, as I do not like marshmallows. I had never tasted a marshmallow, or even touched one, but I knew instinctively that a marshmallow was not for eating. I did not share my distaste for them with Mum. Later she told me that the experiment showed that I could wait for things I really want. I would become very good at waiting.

During one of Nana's visits she offered me a warm cup of cocoa. I eagerly wrapped my hands around the warm mug and I could see the white milky froth as I brought it to my lips and took a long sip. Only, the eagerly anticipated taste of chocolate was overwhelmed by a texture I did not recognise and which I did not like at all. I didn't know it at the time, but submerged beneath the chocolatey surface was a cluster of little white marshmallows. It wasn't long before I knew that my body had encountered something that it was being compelled to purge. I began to vomit.

There are memories of textures and smells that I have grown to love too. The texture of my nana's jam drop biscuit dough as I rolled it in my palms and, with my little floured thumb, gently made an indentation that Nana would fill with raspberry jam. I love the taste and smell of my grampy's chicken soup and how its saltiness always makes me feel better. I also adore the smell of basil. I would sit beside Pa as he picked the basil from his herb garden till the tips of his fingers were stained the colour of tobacco. Pa would blend the ingredients together to make his pesto and I would cook the pasta—the perfect gourmet duet. And this is how Pa and I spent a lot of our time together, in the kitchen. I would watch as he baked biscotti and when it had cooled I would dip one end into a bowl of melted dark chocolate. And he would show me how to preserve lemons in rock salt using recycled jam jars.

Sometimes, cooking with Pa was one of the few things that made sense to me when nothing else seemed to do so.

My mum is the most confident, spirited woman you could ever hope to encounter—or, at times, hope to avoid.

I don't remember when I became aware of my mother's diagnosis. As a child I could not understand the label of schizoaffective disorder. I had not heard of bipolar or the term mental illness. I just knew that there were times when my mother's state of being allowed for wonderful moments of joy and creativity and playfulness. And other times where it overflowed, when her ways of thinking and her erratic behaviour would impact her ability to function at work and at home. And sometimes it was a thief, stealing away her ability to be our mum.

My mother is euphoric, creating and producing, arranging and rearranging, packing and unpacking, sorting and re-sorting random piles of things with a great sense of urgency. My brother and I grew to learn that these piles of things were of the utmost importance. Sometimes when playing we would leap onto one of the piles, sending objects sliding, and we quickly knew we had upset the system and our mother. She would tell us of her perfectly good plan for keeping things in order, and how we had just stuffed it up. In those moments my brother and I became increasingly aware of the 'piles of utmost importance'—even the piles that we could not see, the piles that were watched over by the people that only my mother could see.

My mother was compelled to follow an unpredictable cycle of hypomania and mania. My mother was uninhibited and compulsive and this, combined with a lack of sleep, fed a compulsion to shop, to shop, to shop. My mother would see and hear things that others could not and from this her agitation grew. When she became more unpredictable my brother and I learned to walk on pathways of eggshells, becoming acutely aware of what was around us. There are times when Pa tries to tell my mother what she is doing is not normal. 'Normal,'

FORM

my mother says. 'Whose fucking version of normal do I have to be?'

This cycle of being with its ebbs and flows continued (and continues still), initially with only months in between episodes and later with years as my mother had begun to take lithium.

Lithium is an alkaline earth element that is a key component of lithium-ion batteries. These batteries are long lasting and rechargeable; they are powerful too because they are highly reactive, enabling currents to flow effortlessly. This was my mother when she was manic: she was in a constant state of flux, a flow of continual movement and recharge, of impulsiveness and urgency. She was like a powerful lithium battery, but while the flow fuelled her, it drained us.

Lithium has another form with an opposite effect. Used medicinally in the form of salts, lithium carbonate would significantly reduce the frequency and intensity of my mother's manic episodes. The drug works to quiet my mother's discord and calm her impulsiveness and sense of urgency; it stills her mind. But my mother often laments that lithium alters the colours in her world and dulls her ideas. 'Lithium,' she says, 'makes me so fucking bland.'

Once, when checking in to a flight with a friend, we were asked if we had any lithium batteries in our luggage, and warned that sometimes they catch fire.

As we were walking towards the security gates, my friend asked if I thought a person taking lithium could suddenly burst into flames. I wonder, she said, if your mum could one day just suddenly self-combust.

As a young adult you see your parents through a lens that has been shaped and formed by so many immeasurable small moments from your childhood. And, sometimes in one of those small moments there is an exchange, no, an interchange, from which an understanding emerges. You begin to see your parents from a totally different perspective, as if for the first time.

For me, this moment was when I was thirteen. It was October. I was sitting on a chair in the dining room while my mum kneeled before me. Beside her was a red bucket filled with water, and she was washing and drying my feet. I was calling out for Pa. As he entered the room, he unsuccessfully attempted to avoid the puddles of water splashed across the cork tile floor. But I did not ask if he was okay. I was searching for his feet. Then I saw his painted toenails and I looked at Pa and he nodded his gentle way of knowing. I realised that in this moment my mother was Mary Magdalene. This was the beginning of a manic episode, and already I felt tired.

And for each one of my mother's episodes there usually followed an absence. Pa would tell us she spent most of her time in the mental health unit sleeping. 'It's the medication,' he said. And he would laugh when he told us of her refusal to participate in any group sessions. 'I don't want to hear what's happening in their fucking heads,' she'd say. 'I have enough to listen to in my own.'

And from this came a dichotomy, a division, two versions of me whereby I lived the life of having a mother with episodic mental illness whose coding I could never quite decipher. Nor could I feel its presence until it was there overshadowing our lives at home, leaving me in a constant state of uncertainty until once again it would recede and pass. And at these times I was also a friend, a student, a child, a little girl, who outside of my home life presented myself as being unburdened and carefree.

Mum's absences were always followed by a return. I knew this. And sure enough, one day I would come home from school to find her curled up on the lounge.

'Hey, button,' she would say.

I would snuggle up beside her and inhale the familiar scent of her perfume. She would pat a cushion on her lap and when I lay my head down on it, I would listen as she sang my heart song, 'Dream a Little Dream of Me'.

Once when thinking aloud, a friend of mine asked if I was ever disturbed by the thought that I could 'get' what my mum had. 'You mean, catch it like a cold?' I said.

He sensed I was fearful that my genes would one day betray me. In thinking like this I felt in some way that I was betraying my mama—portraying those aspects of who she was as somehow being less than, as being less than perfect.

But there were moments when I would catch myself laughing too loudly, or for too long. Moments when I was joyful and uninhibited. I would wonder if it was the beginning, the emerging of something that I have always feared.

When I was seventeen, I asked my mum if she thought I could be bipolar, if I had characteristics of schizoaffective disorder. But Mama just shook her head and laughed, loudly. 'Charlotte,' she said, 'you're the sanest one out of the lot of us.' She then reminded me that everyone has their quirks, 'even you,' she said, 'only you do not need to take any medication for yours.' She went on to tell me that a diagnosis doesn't have to define you, it's a part of you but not the whole you. 'It's all about perspective, Charli, you don't look at something from the same angle if you want to try to understand it.'

I had heard of the term 'resilience', but it only resonated with me when I heard the definition of 'extreme resilience'. Extreme resilience has the potential to make someone overly tolerant of unpleasant and counterproductive circumstances and to drive them to persist in pursuing unattainable goals. I can relate to this; I can recognise these traits in the different versions of myself as I have worked to understand who I am.

My mother's episodes were moments of discord that shaped and formed me; some of these moments reverberated loudly and some were so subtle and so quiet that no one could hear their echoes—aside from a child: me. And through my mother's manic episodes, the seeds of resilience were sown and a child of knowing was formed. I began to recognise and more skilfully navigate my mother's manic moments but was yet to understand why they came.

And in these manic moments, a child needs a 'someone' who is a constant, someone stable and sure, someone who will say: 'I know you do not understand some things and I know these things frighten you. I know you want to make things better, but it is not your job to do so. I want you to hear that it is okay to feel these things.'

This someone may be connected to you by blood or by a kinship formed of curdling. And for me, I was blessed to have two such people in my life: my nana and pa, who kept me wrapped in a love made of jam drops and homemade pesto.

I often think about nature and nurture when I wonder how like my mother and father I am. I have one character trait that has been embedded in my being: I am a people-pleaser. I'm just genetically wired that way—like my father. But my formative years were spent with my mother, who can be exceptionally blunt, making statements of facts as she sees them. I wonder if my intense need to please people is a response to this, or in fact a reaction to it. Really, I am a product of both nature *and* nurture, and each has shaped my intense desire to please others.

This tendency was particularly pronounced during my early and late teens, as I floated between different social groups at school, trying desperately to be part of something, trying everything to fit in. I always felt as if I were the odd one out. I was the girl with the 'crazy' mum. I was the girl with 'googly eyes'. I spent almost my entire school life trying to be somebody that I was not, trying to be accepted by people I didn't really like while letting some of my happiest friendships fall by the wayside for fear of what others might think of me. Sadly, I never felt entirely myself in any of my early friendships. I never felt that anyone accepted the whole me, only fragments.

If my character was formed in part as a reaction to my mum's behaviour—nurture—my brother's connection to Mum was one of nature.

We were sitting in the lounge room—me, my mum, Pa and my brother—watching a foreign film. Pa and Mum and I were taking it in turns to read the subtitles out loud, while my brother, like Hephaestus, the god of blacksmiths, used the poker he had fashioned in metalwork at school to nudge another log into the already roaring fire. And he listened to each of us reading, never interrupting. I am not sure exactly why my brother's brain cannot decipher written language; why he can recognise the letters of the alphabet, yet be unable to grasp them once they are put together to form words. My brother seeks knowledge—of metals and rocks, of nature and history and geography—through listening and observing and watching—and talking. My brother is impulsive and unrestrained, just like my mother. There are many moments when the two of them collide, but there are also times when you will find my mum on the phone reading a book aloud to my brother or listening to his latest idea or invention. At other times he'll share a detailed description of the documentary he's currently watching or his theory about the happenings in the world. And there are no interjections accepted, my brother knows himself to be right—he has been a master pupil of my mama.

I got my love of words and books from my mum, so when I was accepted to study media and communications at the University of New South Wales in Sydney, we were both ecstatic.

When I left home Mama gave me an embossed leather journal that fitted in the palm of my hand. In its pages was an inscription: *From the moment you came to be, the first notes of our heart song were being written.* She had composed a heart song, just for me. *You are such a gift, Charlotte. Be true to your heart, love yourself, have the courage to alter paths if you feel lost and choose to dance with those that will nurture you.*

I would chat on the phone with Mum every day and I'd soak up as much as I could about the people, the sounds and the flavours that permeated my patch of Sydney and tell her all about it. But after a few months my world lost its colour and I felt so terribly lost. Even if I'd had the heart to tell her, I couldn't find the words to say how much I hated university. I could not alter my path because I simply did not know how to do it.

fracture

The only obsession everyone wants: love.
People think that in falling in love they make
themselves whole? . . .
I think otherwise. I think you are whole before
you begin. And the love fractures you.
You're whole, and then you're cracked open.

PHILIP ROTH, *THE DYING ANIMAL*

In Sydney, I moved into Grandma's house and worked part-time in my uncle Jason's jewellery shop, which was on the third floor of the Dymocks building on George Street, while I tried without success to embrace university life. I loathed my course; the study was done individually, or in groups in an online format. I felt completely disconnected. Over dinner one evening my godmother, a publicist, listened to my tale of woe. The following week she introduced me to the person who would offer me my first real job—as a publicity and marketing assistant in book publishing. Through my passion for books I found the courage to alter paths, deferring uni and embarking on my wonderful new career. I loved my job but most of all I adored being enveloped by a world of words and books. The financial independence that came with full-time work meant I was able to move into a share house with three friends, including my oldest friend from childhood, Georgia.

The house was a dilapidated terrace on Mary Ann Street in Ultimo and was full of hand-me-down furniture from previous residents, family or friends—or, as was the case for our dining chairs, found on the street outside. There the four of us embarked on the rollercoaster ride of discovery that many people go through in their late teens and early twenties. It was a time of one-night stands, copious amounts of alcohol and spectacularly horrific hangovers, of reckless behaviour, of side-splitting laughter, of themed dress-up house parties. Of late nights spent dancing in the kitchen, singing Adele's 'Someone Like You' so loudly and passionately that we would lose our breath, before happily stuffing our faces on the leftover sausage rolls or chocolate ganache tarts supplied in abundance by Georgia, who worked at Bourke Street Bakery. Of playing pranks on each other and unsuspecting members of the public from the safety and privacy of our enclosed balcony; of bringing what limited groceries our money could buy home in shopping trolleys borrowed from Broadway Shopping Centre.

Of cockroach infestations; of finding fermented potatoes at the back of kitchen cupboards; of being creeped out by our landlord, who would only want to inspect the leaks we reported if one of us was in the shower. Most of all, it was a time of growing up in the company of friends, of watching each other fall in and out of love—with men and women, with jobs, and with ourselves.

But then I met my future husband, and everything changed.

Dating apps didn't exist when we met, so we found each other in the way people don't seem to anymore: two strangers calling out to each other across the bar of the Courthouse Hotel in Newtown.

He was the first proper boyfriend I had ever had, and he was only the second boy to ever take me out to dinner. For our first date, he took me to Lucio Pizzeria in Darlinghurst. I would not recommend pizza as the ideal meal for a first date, it was too stressful. (Do we share or order our own? Should I opt for a white base to avoid the inevitable tomato-to-breast spillage? Do I use a knife and fork or do I pick up the slice and take a bite?) But I was completely smitten by his thick

Groucho Marx moustache and round tortoiseshell glasses. He was charming, like a big beautiful puppy, and he had a contagious love for food. When he ended the night abruptly to go and care for his nonna, promising to cook for me on our second date, I was left hungry for more.

On the second date, in the ramshackle kitchen of my house in Ultimo, he taught me to make bolognese from scratch on the only working element on the stovetop. As I watched in wonder, he sautéed celery, carrot, onion and zucchini in a stock pot with olive oil until they softened. Then he browned some minced meat—a mix of pork and beef—to which he added wine, whole peeled tomatoes, tomato paste and passata. He cooked it low and slow for hours, seasoning it as he went, before serving it alongside pappardelle ribbons and drowning it in grated parmesan cheese.

My palate was so simple, so unsophisticated, that every meal we shared felt like an adventure.

After we had been dating for a month or so, his mother, who had emigrated from Colombia, invited me over for a barbecue to meet their friends and family. I'd studied Italian at high school, but that didn't help at all when it came to understanding their jubilant and fast-paced Spanish. The only word I could grasp—and one which they directed at me repeatedly, was 'Linda'—an ex-girlfriend, no doubt. My pleasure in the homemade beef empanadas, cheese-stuffed corn arepas and mountains of mouth-wateringly chargrilled asado was muted by the constant refrain of her name. 'Linda, Linda, Linda.'

While his mum prepared to serve her famous caramelised flan de leche, I asked to speak to my boyfriend in private. He led me up the stairs to his childhood bedroom with its ceiling covered in painted fluffy clouds, where I demanded to know: 'Who the hell is Linda? Why does everyone keep going on about her?'

He only laughed. *Linda* was the Spanish word for pretty, he explained. They weren't talking about another girl. 'They were talking excitedly about *you*,' he said. 'You are the first girl I have ever brought home.'

Later, when my mum came to Sydney for work, the three of us went to the now-defunct Athenian, a Greek restaurant which occupied a beautiful old bank building in Barrack Street. Stepping through its cavernous, columned entrance was like entering another world, with its interiors and menu remaining steadfastly old school, unchanged for almost two decades. It was my favourite place to go whenever my mama was in town.

As soon as we sat down, my boyfriend immediately tucked his crisp white cotton napkin into his collar like a bib. The three of us shared spit-roasted lamb with tzatziki, spanakopita with flaky fillo pastry, taramasalata and saganaki with freshly toasted pita and creamy, bechamel-laden moussaka. At one point, I looked up to see him smiling widely, engaged in animated conversation with my mum, wearing his food-stained napkin without a shred of self-consciousness, and in that moment I knew I was falling in love with him.

My boyfriend enveloped me in hugs so deep I felt I could drown in them. He was an only child whose dad had passed away too young, and he grew up surrounded by strong and beautiful women—his nonna, his mama and his tia. The great and unconditional love he had received from his mother radiated out of him and into me. He was the only person outside of my family to call me Charli. He was my *guapo*, I was his *guapa*. I was his *gioia mia*—his joy. The sex was wonderful and we were insatiable—for the first couple of years. We were childlike in our sense of play and often laughed, wrestled and mucked around. He loved to travel, lived and breathed by it, and dreamed of travelling to all the countries in Europe before he turned thirty. (He might just have achieved it had it not been for Covid.) He would absorb each and every travel experience, good or bad—he was so open to everything. He had a wealth of useless facts stored in his brain that became useful at the most unexpected times. He had what seemed a pathological love of board games—though it soon became clear that it was not the games themselves that he loved but the *rules*, which he wielded like a dictator. He loved *Mario Kart* and closely resembled the eponymous character. He loved *Tintin* and was thrilled when my father gave us his original poster. He loved puns and was far better at creating them than me. He had an array of coloured t-shirts printed with puns and he paired them with navy blue shorts or long pants and R.M. Williams boots. He made no secret of the fact there was a third party in our relationship: the Wallabies; his love of rugby union verged on an obsession. He loved the colour pink. He had an encyclopaedic knowledge of dogs but didn't yet have one to call his own. He always had to be right, and he wouldn't hesitate in doubling down; I discovered that it was easier just to give in to him. He had so many grown-up aspirations competing with so many boyish desires.

He was passionate about eating food and cooking it. He could look in the fridge and conjure up something delicious from whatever ingredients he found there. He made amatriciana better than I have had in any restaurant. He hated mushrooms, and loathed fish. He didn't believe that soup was a meal. He introduced me to a world of cuisines and flavours

I had never encountered before—Thai, Italian, Spanish, Cuban, Mexican. He rarely drank alcohol. He couldn't stand hot drinks and would never drink coffee.

He could enter a room and talk to *anyone*, about *anything*. He was the kind of person who, on meeting, you felt as though you had always known.

I moved out of Mary Ann Street. After just three months together, we set up our first home, and I thought my life was complete.

In March 2015, after we'd been together for four years, my future husband took me out for dinner at the creative Asian restaurant Ms. G's for my twenty-fourth birthday. As I bit into a cheeseburger spring roll, he told me that he wanted to sleep with other people, that he wanted to 'open up our relationship'.

Shocked, I refused. For the first time in our relationship, I wasn't prepared to just give way. I told him he should talk to someone, a therapist or a counsellor, about his feelings around sex and intimacy. We ate the rest of our meal in silence. *Happy birthday to me.* I haven't been able to stomach a cheeseburger since.

Despite this issue still hanging unresolved between us, we set off in May on a long-planned trip to Europe. We travelled together to Iceland, inspired by Hannah Kent's novel *Burial Rites*. I saw a landscape covered in snow for the first time and frozen waterfalls and icebergs that filled the sea like ships. We went hunting for the bones of abandoned planes and bogged our once-white, uninsured rented Renault in thick black sand, only to be rescued by a monster truck driven by a man named Thor.

From there we flew to the Faroe Islands, where we had no other option but to eat like locals—devouring raw sea urchin and langoustine that had been harvested fresh from the roaring ocean that morning. We ate whale steaks and wind-dried fermented lamb that smelled (and tasted) like rotting flesh. We took a small boat across the roughest of seas to visit a remote island where puffins build their nests on the cliff's edge.

We travelled to Bologna and met Georgia for a weekend of absolute gluttony. We began at my favourite restaurant there, Da Silvio, where, rather than ordering from the menu, we sat back and placed ourselves in the chef's hands. First, the antipasti arrived with an assortment of ten or so dishes designed to share. We feasted on fried polenta served in a rich tomato sauce; slices of mortadella with a velvety mortadella mousse; a creamy local burrata; grilled asparagus in extra virgin olive oil and an entire wheel of pecorino—which was left on our table for us. Then came the pasta course. There was bolognese, of course, plus a dish of potato gnocchi tossed in pesto and tortellini sautéed in a sage butter sauce. We were then presented with the most magnificent osso buco, the braised veal shanks so tender and so succulent that we wished we had left room for more. But the tour de force was dessert. Ten individual offerings were brought to the table— not to select from, but to devour in their entirety. A decadent chocolate torte; zuppa inglese; tiramisu; homemade gelato; almond biscotti; a rich, thick chocolate sauce to pour over fluffy meringues; a blueberry crostata. To accompany the food we were generously served prosecco, lambrusco, barbera, trebbiano, sangiovese and, as a *digestivo*, ice-cold limoncello.

The uncertainty I'd felt before we left home was banished; being in love, and hungry, was addictive. But not long after we returned to Australia in August, he returned to *that* conversation, repeating that he wanted to sleep with other people. At our favourite cafe, West Juliett, over French toast served with vanilla poached pears and a thick caramel sauce, he ended our relationship. The timing couldn't have been worse for me.

I was due to leave for the airport later that day to accompany an author on a three-week national publicity tour. Despite the fact that the bottom had fallen out of my world, I had no option but to go to the airport as planned.

It wasn't until much later that night, in a hotel room in another city, I realised there had been no conversation, that he made his decision on his own. And I texted him, desperate.

> My brain wasn't registering what you were saying . . . that you were leaving me.
> And I'm here now thinking that I didn't say to you that I wanted you to stay.
> That I didn't want you to leave. I don't want you to leave.
> I just need to tell you that I don't want you to leave. Please don't leave.

He responded minutes later.

> I need to do this for myself. I know it sucks right now (because it hurts for me too) but I need this. I need to go be independent for a while. I think the independence will make me love what we have even more and appreciate it more. I take the risk that you may not want to be with me in the future but I also take the risk that by not doing this I'm not being true to myself. I want to one day continue

this relationship if you are keen for that at the time. Right now it's not what I want and I'm so sorry I can't give you what you want.

Distraught, I called my mama. She dropped everything and followed me across the country on my work trip. She drove for hours to meet me in Brisbane, where she would wait for me in my hotel room while I went and did my job. And in the evening, when the hotel room door closed, she was there. I couldn't sleep, missing my ex-boyfriend beside me in my bed. Mum, realising this, bought me a huggable hippo pillow, it was hairy, a comforter for children. I buried my face in its soft velvety fur and imagined I was resting my head on my ex-boyfriend's hairy chest. It felt like home to me.

But then I felt my eyes and my face begin to tingle and burn. I looked at Mum. 'Fucking cats,' she said, and the next minute we were running to find a pharmacy. I'm allergic to cats, you see—or, more precisely, I have an allergy to a particular protein in cat saliva that sticks to their fur when they lick themselves. By the time we exited the lift my mouth had swollen so much that when I tried to talk drool ran down the side of my chin. I was finding it hard to see out of my left eye, and Mum, well, she couldn't stop laughing. I don't know why we laugh when awful things happen, but we do, and in our family, with everything that happens, there's a *lot* of laughing.

The pharmacist asked what had happened and he looked at Mum for an explanation but I did not need to look as I knew immediately what she had done. Rather than buy the hippo pillow brand new, she'd gone op-shopping, and I had been hugging an unwashed pillow covered in its previous owner's cat's hair. I told Mum that she'd nearly killed me and she said she was happy that all my years in drama classes had not gone to waste. This was *so* Mum. Imperfectly perfect. I forgot how sad I was and laughed out loud.

While I was busy with work, my boyfriend moved out of our house on Blackwattle Bay, quit his job and flew to Europe to find himself.

Georgia agreed to move in. *Counting down the days till we are naked in the same house again*, she texted me. She brought hope and humour in a dark, lonely time.

At the end of October, my ex-boyfriend messaged to say that he missed me, not just as his girlfriend but as his friend. *I still love you incredibly*, he said. He told me that he had been thinking about what I had said in March about him seeing a therapist to discuss his issues around intimacy and sex and that he would consider it when he returned.

> You have the biggest place in my heart and you always
> have. I never stopped loving you. And I never said I
> have or I would. I broke up with you for very selfish
> reasons and that you are still talking to me is a testament
> of your character.

Mama came down to Sydney to care for me when I needed to have my wisdom teeth removed. The extraction went fine but then I experienced 'dry sockets', a condition so painful I was given Endone, and because I'd never really had any kind of drug other than Panadol I reacted badly. I was outside the dental surgery when he called. With my gums stuffed with cloves and my brain in a fog, I'd finally had enough.

'I can't be the one to listen to you sort yourself out,' I told him. 'You haven't changed a bit since you left almost two months ago. I deserve so much more. You are free to sleep with whoever you want. I have no desire or need to know. We are not a couple; you're entitled to do whatever you want to do.'

'My heart aches,' he replied. 'I'm sorry. I'll leave you be.'

Baking became a form of therapy for me. It was meditative. It created a sense of calm, a sense of order. It forced me to drill down and focus. At a time when it seemed like nothing was certain, baking became my one certainty. I knew that if I made a slow and deliberate effort to follow a recipe to the letter, I would be rewarded with a delicious, sugar-filled mouthful of instant gratification within the hour.

Over those months of heartbreak, I baked everything and anything: juicy apple crumble, fragrant banana bread, vanilla-poached pears, pavlova, triple chocolate ice-cream sandwiches, pear and rhubarb muffins, tangy baked cheesecakes, roasted hazelnut tortes, and the fluffiest vanilla sponge layered with jam and cream. I learned that salt is the secret ingredient, not only to chocolate chip cookies and caramel slice, but to freshly cut oranges, too. In the heat of summer, I became enamoured with roasted stone fruit. I would halve peaches, plums, nectarines and apricots, scraping vanilla bean seeds over them and drizzling them with honey before baking them at 180°C for twenty or so minutes, until softened. I would serve them with cream or ice cream for dessert, or have them for breakfast with muesli, natural yoghurt and more honey.

Back then, baking was one of the only times—perhaps *the* only time—that I found myself present in my own body, with my mind completely clear. It was such a sensory experi-ence—of touch, of texture, of smell, of taste—that I became instantly grounded. It reminded me of how I used to bake jam drops with my nana, giving me a sense of security when I felt adrift. To this day, whenever I beat butter and sugar I still dip my finger into the mixture to taste, and in that tiny morsel of batter I find myself sitting on the counter in Nana's kitchen, my little legs swinging, licking the beaters of her old Kenwood mixer clean. Nan used to say that I put more batter into my mouth than into the biscuits themselves, and that has never really changed.

J ust before Christmas, my ex-boyfriend returned to Australia and sent me a flurry of Facebook messages.

I can give you what you want.

After we last spoke I really took the time to look at myself and what I wanted. It became clearer as the days went on. And I'm sure now more than ever. I want you in my life. And I want to be in yours.

I don't want to just be in it—I want to be a great part of your life. To share great moments with you.

> I feel a mix of good feelings. Love for you. Excitement
> to see you/talk to you/look into your eyes. And also
> nervousness. I'm really fearful that you hate me. And
> most of all I feel vulnerable. In both a good and a bad
> way. I'm offering myself to you on a plate.

I was overwhelmed. I didn't reply initially. It was everything I
had been longing to hear and my first instinct was to run into
the comfort and familiarity of his arms, of his smell. But I
wasn't sure I could trust his change of heart.

He wrote again.

> I just feel like I'm in limbo with you until you know what
> you want. My heart hurts just thinking that maybe I've
> missed my chance with you.

I messaged him then, telling him that I would like to see
him. He arrived with a small box, gift-wrapped. I opened it
to discover a Nikon camera, just like my papa used to have.
I was moved by the thoughtful present, but I needed more
time to think about what I wanted.

My mum messaged me as I was about to board a flight on
my way to see her for Christmas.

> Remember, Charlotte, whatever you decide to do make
> sure you sow new healthy seeds to grow the things

you want—don't just pick through the soil and try to reinvigorate the old seeds. You'll just get the same crop.

On Christmas Eve, he wrote:

> I hope you are having a nice evening wherever you are. Wishing you were here. Please know that no matter how you feel towards me, if you think you will be able to trust me or not, that I'll not be angry at you and that I'll always want you to be happy. Even if that means without me. I'll still love you.

For Christmas lunch, Grampy and I donned coloured crowns. Mama made spinach pie in *the* spinach pie dish, and my pa made moussaka. Grampy stuffed snapper with lemon and dill and baked it in alfoil. There was ham off the bone, prawns, steamed potatoes, a Greek salad with crumbled feta and steamed green beans. Desserts were my domain; I made a pavlova covered in a precarious tower of whipped cream and vanilla bean and topped with mango, nectarine and passionfruit. Three mouthfuls in, my phone buzzed. I looked down at it to find he had sent another text:

Sometimes you forget that I'm mad about you.

I spent New Year's Eve with my best friend on Blackwattle Bay. We drank French champagne and nibbled on crackers topped with brie and quince paste as the sun set. For dinner we roasted lamb and served it on a bed of creamy polenta with a side of steamed broccolini. Midnight was bittersweet; instead of kissing my ex-boyfriend, I curled up in bed alone.

At the beginning of the new year, without telling anyone, I snuck away with him to Kangaroo Valley for a weekend to reconnect. We slept in separate beds, we did not have sex, but together we began to rebuild what was lost. I was still anxious, though, still cautious. Yet, despite my trepidation, I wanted him. I wanted him in a way that I knew would wound me.

Telling him that I thought we should take our time, I threw myself into work. I went on a business trip to London, where I spent every spare minute exploring the feast for the senses that is travelling solo for the first time. I explored Borough Market, licking vanilla custard and cinnamon sugar from my fingers after demolishing a Bread Ahead doughnut. I devoured a bacon-and-egg naan at Dishoom and made myself eat some Ottolenghi salads to offset the cakes and tarts and cookies I ate there too. For my twenty-fifth birthday, my friend Amelia, who was living in Ireland at the time, met me at St Pancras Station and we took the Eurostar together to Paris. We ate wafer-thin crepes slathered in Nutella, potato rosti and runny eggs at Holybelly, and cheese platters at Le Comptoir, where the well-known Australian chef Bill Granger happened to be seated beside us. We sipped Kir Royales and savoured butterscotch macaroons in St Germain, and Amelia selflessly joined me for my favourite meal of steak frites (she, a devout vegetarian, could only eat the frites). We ate our weight in pastries and croissants from Du Pain et des Idées and drank champagne with a view of the Eiffel Tower.

When I returned to Australia in April I moved into a new house, directly across the road from my old one, and my boyfriend moved in too. But this time around, I was determined not to lose sight of myself. Previously, I had always put his needs, his interests, first, which left me with very little energy for my own. But now I wanted to ensure that I carved out space for myself and the things I loved doing, or at least that was the plan. During our break, baking had been my mainstay, and as I grew ever more passionate about it I decided I wanted to share the results with others. Using the camera he had given me for Christmas, I began photographing my baking creations and uploading them to Instagram. Gratified by the response, I self-published an ebook, *Bakeree*, which included recipes that would later form part of my first published book, *Just Desserts*. Gradually, though, buoyed by the reactions of others to my efforts, I stopped baking for myself and began baking for others. I baked carrot cake with caramelised pecans for my friend Rob, one of the first people I met when I moved to Sydney, to nurse him through a break-up, and a dark chocolate torte for my friend Ali to celebrate her new job. I craved their affirmation, their compliments. They lifted me up, making me feel appreciated, in a way doing something purely for myself didn't. I no longer ate what I baked and instead began nurturing and nourishing my loved ones, even strangers, baking extravagant, time-intensive desserts for them. But as time passed, where once baking had calmed and centred me, it was now anxiety-inducing. I found myself unable to say no when I was asked to bake for birthdays, office events, engagement parties, even weddings. I would finish twelve-hour workdays, sometimes landing back in Sydney late at night from a trip interstate, and have to bake something I had committed myself to delivering the next day. My stress levels were peaking as I stepped outside of, and turned away from, myself once more. A pattern began to emerge. I would find things I was good at, throw myself into them, give my all and lose my sense of self entirely.

Meanwhile, the drive and ambition I brought to my work and extracurricular projects only highlighted my boyfriend's lack of direction. While from the outside we looked like a couple on the same page, inside I could feel the gulf between us widening—and I was desperate to hold things together.

We became engaged over a game of hangman. No bended knee, no ring, no fanfare. We were in the Hunter Valley for my twenty-sixth birthday and it was raining non-stop. At the house where we were staying was a chalkboard wall; we'd been playing hangman all weekend. We had talked about marriage intermittently and were asked about it often by others, given how long we'd been together, but it had become clear that marriage wasn't something he was interested in, and certainly wasn't something he would ever initiate. I, on the other hand, had long had a picture in my head of how my life was *supposed* to play out. I was in a serious relationship at nineteen and had been promoted to a senior management position in my company by twenty-three; I was now determined to be married by twenty-seven, with babies before I turned thirty. So, in a fleeting moment of clarity—perhaps subconsciously inspired by my mama's own spontaneous proposal to Pa— over fourteen blank spaces, and in three sweet guesses, he puzzled out <u>W</u> <u>I</u> <u>L</u> <u>L</u> <u>Y</u> <u>O</u> <u>U</u> <u>M</u> <u>A</u> <u>R</u> <u>R</u> <u>Y</u> <u>M</u> <u>E</u> and avoided the hangman's noose.

He looked at the chalkboard, looked at me, and said aloud: 'Well, will you marry me?'

I said yes. Even though I'd initiated the proposal, I was completely taken by surprise. I never thought he would actually *say* the words; I thought he would roll his eyes and shrug it off and we would make a joke of it all. But he didn't.

There is a part of me that now feels like, by forcing his hand, I cheated myself out of a proper proposal—a proposal that meant something. It was all done so halfheartedly. Perhaps that was why we drank our champagne in silence. Perhaps that was why we didn't make any phone calls or public announcements and waited weeks, even months, to sheepishly tell family we were engaged. It could also have had something to do with the fact that getting married was based on a series of compromises. The two biggest compromises were that I was to learn how to drive (which I didn't, and still do not know how to do) and I was also to begin sharing my bank accounts with him—which my mama told me never to do but I agreed to anyway, forgoing my financial independence blindly. Something I would later come to deeply regret.

We were married on 26 May 2018 at Wallalong House, a stunning 1800s farmhouse in the Hunter Valley. In many ways I was going through the motions; I think we both were. We walked down the aisle—he arm in arm with his mama and me escorted by my beloved pa—as Georgia sang Bob Marley's 'Is This Love'. I did not wear white, instead I wore a colourful tulle gown from Temperley London, which I had fallen in love with years before our engagement. Inspired by the incomparable Frida Kahlo and our travels in Mexico back in 2013, the dress featured delicately hand-painted florals in euphorically bright colours stitched onto ivory silk. The florals crept over long, sheer sleeves towards a nipped-in waist and a floor-length fitted skirt. Our rings were handmade and designed by my uncle Jason and gifted to us by my grandma. The day was bright and beautiful, full of colour and endless potential—and so, it seemed, was our future.

The ceremony took place under the shade of two towering two-hundred-year-old fig trees and, after eight years together, I saw my husband cry for the first time as he read his vows to me. We cut the cake, a lemon dream made by Nadine Ingram of the iconic Woolloomooloo bakery Flour and Stone—layers of lemon butter cake, meringue, lemon curd and double cream—as Nick Cave's 'Into My Arms' played. It was one of nine wedding cakes we had on the day, with the other creations being Nadine's chocolate, raspberry and buttercream cake; brown butter tart; carrot cake; tiered chocolate cake; pistachio, raspberry and rose cake; hazelnut torte; panna cotta lamington; salted caramel and chocolate tart and, to finish, an old-fashioned vanilla sponge cake. I don't know if Amelia and Ali will ever forgive me for putting them in charge of those cakes; it was perhaps the most stressful hour of their lives, transferring such precious cargo from cake box to cake stand.

During their speech, Mama and Pa surprised me by calling up the village—godparents, childhood friends, family friends, neighbours—that had helped to raise me, and together they sang Archie Roach's 'Love in the Morning'. We had our first dance (an uncoordinated shuffle) to Jimmy Fontana's 'Il Mondo', and as the champagne and tears and laughter flowed, our friend Declan wheeled out an ice-cream cart filled with offerings from Gelato Messina. I am proud to say that our family and friends demolished two hundred and eighty scoops of gelato and devoured every single last crumb of cake.

One day you're planning a wedding and the next you're packing a suitcase. Our honeymoon in Japan—the first time either of us had visited the country—was the sort of trip that a foodie's dreams are made of.

We landed in Tokyo and discovered that, in Japan, queuing is an artform; all the best places to eat involved a wait. We waited patiently outside Udon Shin, a hole-in-the-wall restaurant in Tokyo's Shinjuku ward, mesmerised by the balletic movements of the chef's hand making the thick and chewy noodles while we waited. I ordered their carbonara-inspired udon, which came topped with a knob of butter, cracked black pepper, freshly grated parmesan and a thick wedge of crispy tempura bacon.

Tokyo's dessert scene was mouth-wateringly good, too. Sunday Bake Shop's owner, Kazuko, well and truly stole my heart. I sat on a little wooden bench in the corner of her bustling and beautiful bakery to get my morning sugar fix and devoured the most amazing cheesecake.

From Tokyo we travelled to the beautiful onsen town of Shuzenji. The area was a treat to explore, with gorgeous rivers running through and hot pools in which to bathe your feet. Somehow, we were the only Westerners in sight. My husband noticed a tiny ramshackle bamboo hut on the side of a dirt road we were walking down and insisted we step inside. We found ourselves the only customers, occupying two of the ten plastic stools surrounding the kitchen run by chef Sakuza-san. The only English words spoken were 'super delicious soba'. Prepared before our eyes, our first course consisted of cold soba noodles with sea salt and freshly grated wasabi. Our second course was cold soba noodles with broth, tempura, seaweed flakes and shallots.

Anthony Bourdain passed away during our time in Osaka. This led me to begin watching his TV series *No Reservations*, starting with the episode in which he explores that vibrant, food-obsessed city, which he referred to as 'the kitchen or belly of Japan'. Something that really struck me (and has stuck with me) at the beginning of the episode was a word that essentially summed up our time in Japan—and, really, sums up almost every single travel experience I have ever had: *kuidaore*. Essentially, it means to eat oneself into total ruin; to eat oneself into bankruptcy. I don't regret a minute of it.

Our honeymoon was magical. I came home feeling more in love than I had in a very long time.

While the wedding and honeymoon had brought us closer together, a return to everyday life saw the romance fade, and two major points of contention emerged.

The first of these was money.

The one stipulation my husband had when getting married was that he would be in charge of managing our finances but in hindsight I know what he was actually seeking was complete control of our finances. His demand seemed to have originated from a completely unfounded contention on his part that, while I was very good at earning money—in fact, I earned considerably more than he did—I was terrible at managing it. (I had once described to him how my mother had episodes of compulsive shopping and I wondered if he was now projecting my mother's behaviours onto me—he wouldn't have been the first, nor the last, to do so.)

When one of our wedding guests gave us a gift of a signed copy of *The Barefoot Investor* by Scott Pape, my husband treated that book like a bible—it was the gospel truth, and he lived his life according to Pape's teachings. He had grand dreams, with schemes to buy multiple houses and become a property magnate, the end goal being to retire by the time he turned forty. But I wondered if he really wanted to do the work required to get there. Rather than earning the money himself to fulfil his ambitions, he instead became frugal with the money I was making, which was now being paid into our joint bank account.

In line with the financial plan he had devised, our money was divided into tiers—or 'buckets', as Pape refers to them. The main 'everyday' account would be used for our rent, an approved list of groceries (always bought from Aldi, never from Harris Farm), petrol, public transport, electricity, phone bills, the internet and streaming subscriptions. I was often derided for not transferring money into the correct 'bucket', I'd face relentless questioning over each and every transaction, with receipts for all purchases carefully scrutinised, and I would be repeatedly reminded that I had not requested his approval before spending—even on necessary shared groceries. I was allocated $100 a week with which to cover anything beyond what he deemed was a necessary expenditure. I struggled to keep my husband's increasing obsession with saving money and the subsequent control of my spending hidden from family and friends. There were moments when I'm sure they silently queried why I couldn't go out for dinner or a show or buy a bottle of wine. My husband even insisted that our rare date nights be paid for out of our personal allowances. I knew that the situation I was in was not normal when I needed to buy new bras. Weeks before I planned to buy them, I began to state my case in my head. When I approached him to ask for additional funds, I thought I had prepared for every possible rebuttal, but what I hadn't anticipated was his outright refusal. Even more concerning was the fact that I accepted this without protest.

Though, there were moments when I stood my ground, such as when I insisted that I had a right to access my money to pay for sessions with my psychologist each month. And then, as the fault line between us widened, when I was starting to question whether I should stay in my marriage or run from it and I knew I needed more support, I began to divert funds so that I could increase my sessions with my psychologist from monthly to fortnightly. And it was only then that I could begin to see the cost of not being in control of financial decisions and how this was impacting on my sense of wellbeing. How giving another person—even one I loved and trusted—absolute dominance over my financial self-sufficiency was forcing me to become secretive. It made me feel immense shame.

I should make it clear that I *did* have access to our joint account. It's just that I couldn't bring myself to touch it. The barrage of questions that would result, the cross-examining of my every monetary decision, eroded my self-confidence to a point where I began to doubt my own competence and it was easier just to accede to the demands. Thus, through my silence, I became unintentionally complicit in my own financial manipulation.

I am embarrassed now by how I let this happen, but it is more common than you might imagine. When our marriage ended, and I finally regained control over my own money and I had the freedom to buy myself whatever I wanted, I bought the most beautiful bra I could find—and I didn't keep the receipt.

The second issue besetting our marriage was sex.

We were together for almost ten years in total. And as the end of that decade neared, it dawned on me that our futile attempts to sustain our relationship masked the constant arguing and deluge of criticism that only served to put a strain on our desire for one another. For me, it seemed like we had drifted away from being lovers and found ourselves in a relationship that was more familial. I felt like I was mothering him—and as psychologist Esther Perel says, mothering is loving, but it is hardly sexy.

But for my husband, sex was how he showed love and how he felt loved. Sex helped to alleviate his anxiety—but became a source of mine. For the first time, I realised how I had become a chronic accommodator in the bedroom. I needed to find my voice to say no to sex when I didn't want it. On reflection, I can only imagine how hurtful it must have been for my husband to be constantly dismissed and rejected by me. He took it to mean that I didn't desire him.

Instead of sharing his concerns, he went on the attack, telling me one night that I had never satisfied him sexually. At that moment I hated him, but I hated myself more because I believed him; I knew it to be true. His constant desire to sleep with other women before we married was proof of this. Even after our marriage he was quite open about his lust for other women, telling me that he wished he could have sex with them. Of course, this only reinforced my sense of inadequacy, of never being enough.

I know now that my inability to articulate my needs came from a lifetime of trying to please other people, to become what they wanted me to be. At the time, though, I could only see the ways in which I was undesirable, unworthy, and not enough.

And I knew this was no way to be in a marriage. I knew this was no way to live.

My husband and I first attended couples therapy in March 2019, some nine months after our wedding day. The office of the woman I came to think of as the Guide was tucked behind a bookshop on the North Shore, and we would meet her every second Thursday at 7.30 am. We went to her hoping that she would help us return to ourselves, and to each other. No matter how tired or hungover I was, or how irritable we were with one another, we never missed an appointment.

The Guide was tall, slim, dark-haired, perfectly manicured and impeccably dressed with a wide smile displaying the whitest of teeth. She was warm and welcoming, and was able to lull both of us into a strange sense of comfort on an incredibly uncomfortable couch. I always sat on the right, he on the left, and at the beginning of every session there was a cavernous space between us that seemed to close ever so slightly as we painstakingly worked our way through the hour.

If I am honest with myself, as much as I desperately wanted our marriage to work, I knew that I couldn't discover who I was, the real me, if I was also treading water in a futile effort to keep my relationship from drowning. This might explain why, around the same time that our couples therapy sessions commenced, I also started inspecting apartments to rent. I was trying to walk away and hold on at the same time.

Still, we limped along, though soon even the things that had bound us together became sites of conflict—including food and cooking. My husband's need for control and dominance extended to the kitchen, which he considered his domain. On the rare occasions I did cook, I became so sensitive to his constant criticism that preparing even the smallest and most simple of meals became a cause of heated friction.

One time I worked up the courage to make Marion Grasby's delightfully uncomplicated Sichuan beef pepper noodles. It was my first attempt at cooking something new and not out of a packet for my husband, and I was determined to impress him. A dish that should have taken just thirty minutes to prepare took me hours, I was so intent on serving up the perfect dinner.

I carried the dishes to the table and, even before I'd sat down, my husband took a mouthful and said, 'I don't like it.'

I laughed, thinking he must be joking.

'Try it!' he said.

As soon as my fork touched my lips (I didn't yet know how to use chopsticks), I felt a tingling sensation. This was followed by an uncomfortable numbness. Horrified, I realised that I had accidentally added two *tablespoons* of Sichuan peppercorns to the dish instead of two teaspoons. The dinner was inedible. My husband didn't bother to conceal his contempt. As I cried into my noodles he gave me some advice that humiliated me at the time, but which has stood me in good stead ever since: you must always *always* read the recipe twice before beginning, and you must always taste what you are cooking as you go.

While this advice would turn out to be valuable, he delivered it with an air of irritating authority. Our relationship had deteriorated to the point where instead of encouraging me, he often belittled me, focusing on my shortcomings. He would assert with certainty any perceived deficits he had noted in my cooking and I became almost paralysed in the kitchen. While I lost my ability to make a savoury meal, I never lost my love of baking. In this arena, I never relinquished my control.

With my married life being anything but loving and har-monious, I was excited to be going home to my mama's house for Christmas with my husband and mother-in-law. There, I knew, I could bask in the warmth of people who loved me and finally relax, if only for a few days. But when we arrived on Christmas Eve it was to find that there was no tree and no decorations, only a large plastic flamingo wrapped in red tinsel with a Santa's hat perched on its head. There were no presents and my mother had done no meal planning or shopping for the twenty or so people she was planning on hosting. My anger and frustration were tempered by the haunting realisation that my mother was not well. What followed was a major manic episode, which I had not experienced since moving out of home.

From my perspective—a selfish one, I know—the timing of this episode could not have been worse. I was on the verge of ending my marriage, wrestling with anxiety and guilt and indecision, and Mum's illness meant that my most important confidante wasn't available to me. And as much as I wanted to tell her everything I was thinking and feeling, I didn't want to add to her burden.

In the absence of my mum, I longed for food that would remind me of her, food that would take me home—scents rising from my kitchen that would transport me back to my childhood. Like her creamy rice, a recipe my nana gave to my mama and my mama to me. When I was little, I would watch her make it: stirring the delightfully comforting combination of arborio rice, full-cream milk, demerara sugar and vanilla on the stovetop. She would then top *half* of it with grated nutmeg—leaving the other half plain, because she knew I didn't like nutmeg—and put it in the fridge to chill. We devoured it cold by the bowlful.

But most of all, I craved the things she rarely made: those dishes reserved for special occasions, like birthdays or Christmas. There was her moussaka, made from a recipe in the stained, dog-eared, sauce-splattered pages of Tess Mallos's *Greek Cookbook*, which Mama and Pa have used throughout their twenty-eight years together. I longed to have this book for myself, but it had long been out of print. Then one serendipitous day, while browsing amongst the thousands of second-hand books crammed into every corner and crevice of Gould's Bookshop on King Street in Newtown, I found it. There was the moussaka recipe on page 58, the very one I grew up eating. In neat blue cursive the previous book's owner had suggested replacing the moussaka's traditional creamy bechamel sauce with 'a carton of plain yoghurt'—something I have been reluctant to try.

No matter how many times I have set out to make it, though, my moussaka never tastes as good as Mum's. I think it has something to do with the special dish she bakes it in.

Actually, I *know* it does. For me, the beauty of moussaka lies within that rich, red, Italian terracotta Mamma Rò dish of hers.

There is also my most treasured recipe of all: Mama's spinach pie. It has become a tangible and edible reminder of her love for me, a powerful dose of nostalgia. I would make it often in those agonising weeks of deciding whether or not to dismantle my life, piece by painful piece. I would find solace in the process of stripping silverbeet leaves from their stalks, steaming them and squeezing out any excess moisture. I would crumble salty Dodoni feta into a creamy mixture of eggs, ricotta and dill, adding onions and shallots that had been caramelised in extra virgin olive oil. I would melt butter and brush it generously between layers of paper-thin fillo pastry that hung over the side of the baking dish, alternating the direction with every second sheet. Like making pasta dough, layering this pie was ritualistic, therapeutic. I would bake it until it was golden brown, and then serve it straight from the oven with buttered potatoes and green beans. A hug in every mouthful.

As my relationship with my husband became more stifling, I found I needed more intensive support, just for me. I am eternally grateful to the Guide who pointed me in the direction of a new psychologist, the Oracle. After almost a decade of being in and out of therapist's offices, never quite finding a match, I found *her*. The one. She changed everything for me, just when I needed her the most. Her little sun-kissed office, located in a quiet pocket of the city, became my refuge, a safe space to call my own. A safe space to retreat to, in which I finally felt seen and heard. Even though there were some thirty years between us, we had something very important in common. The Oracle's mother, too, had bipolar disorder, and she was able to help me to separate my mama from her illness.

She also urged me to write, assuring me that it would help me to express myself. With her encouragement, I first put pen to paper and began to keep a journal. I wrote my first entry in January 2020.

> *I have never kept a journal before.*
> *I hope I can look back at this and read how brave, strong and determined I was.*
> *But right now, I can barely even recognise myself.*

I was finding it harder and harder to breathe in my marriage. What I really needed was the time and space in which to think: about myself, about us, about the future and what I wanted that to look like. So, after many sessions with the Oracle, I worked up the courage to ask my husband for a trial separation. However, he made it clear that if I left, it wouldn't be a separation but a divorce. It was an ultimatum. 'I'm telling you that the separation is final for me. That I can't go back and forth. You're taking it as a threat,' he said. And he was right, I was feeling threatened. I was a woman under siege.

I am often asked if there was an exact moment: a moment when I knew that I was going to leave my husband. I have always been reluctant to answer, because of course the decision to leave is born of many moments. Instead, I speak not of a moment but a belief: that life could be better; that I could be happier. But the truth is there was a moment, a specific moment, when I knew I had to leave because, if I didn't, I would lose sight of myself entirely.

To further supplement our income, I had started a side gig as a content creator developing recipes. In late February I met my husband in Pyrmont, where we were to board a boat—well, a superyacht—as part of a promotional perk for a job I had just done for an ice-cream company. We were surrounded by bottles of Moët on ice, caviar by the bowlful and a delightful saxophonist who was bringing more energy to his fifteen minutes of fame than I had allowed myself to muster in months. (In fact, there is very little enthusiasm I can muster when it comes to caviar—I simply don't get it.)

I was there on that boat with my husband, but I wasn't there. Not really. Instead of revelling in the glamour of the occasion, I was weighed down by the stress of a secret I had been keeping from him. I had been paid my work bonus the week prior and, instead of putting it in our joint account, I had deposited it into a new bank account I had opened without his knowledge. I was so bound by the financial constraints he had devised that I felt compelled to reveal my hidden money to him, but I also had to tell him what I wanted to do with that money.

The yacht cruised from Pyrmont to Mosman, where it turned. As the sun set over the Sydney Harbour Bridge, I worked up the courage to tell him that my bonus had come through. 'I'd like to use it to take a sabbatical in Paris,' I said. It was something I had always dreamed of doing.

He just smiled and shook his head. 'You know, I would *really* love for you to have Paris, but that money has to go straight into our savings, for our house deposit.'

That was *the* moment. The moment that it dawned on me that my soul would not survive if I stayed in this marriage; that I would never be able to live the life I wanted, never be able to pursue my aspirations, as long as we were together. I remember looking at him, a chill coming over me as the sun sank below the horizon, and despite the darkness, there was light. A sense of hope. And a belief that I could do this. That I could take control of my life.

I didn't expect that his heart would break when I told him in our kitchen later that night, sitting on the countertop, that I was leaving our marriage. I didn't anticipate his tears, or that he would beg me to stay. I didn't foresee him promising to change, to work on himself, to *finally* seek out individual therapy, which he had promised to consider all those years ago. But I am proud of my head for maintaining sovereignty when all my heart wanted was for those words to be true.

I wrote in my journal:

Money! For the first time in two years I have my own money again!

I summoned the courage to explain to my friends what I had been going through—and for the first time I asked for help. That might sound like a small thing, but for me it was profound. I've never liked to ask for anything; in my friendships, I've always tried to put myself in the role of caregiver because I want to be needed. So much of my identity was defined by looking after people. But I now know that in any relationship—not just friendships—it's okay to ask for help, to ask for your needs to be met, too.

Nearly a year after we first began seeing the Guide, I emailed her to let her know that the session we'd had the morning prior to going on the yacht would be our last.

She wrote back immediately.

> Putting your needs as a priority and not self-sacrificing in order to hang on to a relationship is also a position of respect and care—for yourself but also for the dignity of the other person. It may not feel that way for you both right now but is a longer-term possibility. Uncoupling is a big process. Take your time and take care. Keep communicating and keep your sense of self.

I had thought that in finally making a decision—the decision to leave—I had escaped an inevitable suffocation, but I was riddled with doubt, saturated in shame and consumed by the hauntings of failure, of a failed marriage. I was afraid of the inevitable voices of disappointment and condemnation—most of which were in my own head.

fade

*The story of my life is wanting, hungering, for what
I cannot have or, perhaps, wanting what I dare not
allow myself to have.*

ROXANE GAY, *HUNGER*

As I have grown older, I have come to understand that there are many kinds of love—a love for a parent, a sibling, a partner and a love for a friend. Each kind of love brings its own light and darkness—and heartbreak.

I met my best friend when I was sixteen. She became like a sister to me; she was *my* person.

While in some ways we were incredibly similar, the differences between us were vast. She lived life with just what she needed, never to excess or for show. She was the type of person who would make you a birthday card rather than buy one because cards and words were what mattered most to her. Photographs mattered, too. She would obsessively document each and every moment with her petite Nikon J5 camera (the same as my own), and was always running out of storage on her ageing Mac as a result. She had a bottomless stomach—perhaps the most wonderful quality in a friend that the feeder in me could have asked for. She was vegetarian but hated zucchini. She relished routine. She loved to walk everywhere. She was never on time. Her fingers and wrists were laden with the silver jewellery she had collected throughout her travels over the years. It jingled when she walked so you would always know when she was approaching. She loved beer but wasn't fond of bubbles and she only drank in moderation. She was always in control. She was worldly and wise and kind. She was always present—in every conversation, in every interaction.

She had known my husband since they were children, their mothers being incredibly close friends—both had migrated to Australia from Colombia. Her heart, and soul, belonged in London and, until Covid forced her return, she had lived there on and off for the past five years.

She had access to parts of me that nobody else had ever had. I considered her to be one of my greatest loves. And when we found ourselves in Morocco's Atlas Mountains, watching the sun set over the Agafay Desert, I told her as much: 'You are the greatest love of my life,' I said. I could tell she was taken aback by my declaration. I had said something she could not say back, something that I could not take back, something that she didn't quite understand. But she was someone whom I knew I could trust implicitly, who would love me unconditionally, no matter what. That was what I did: I told her *everything*. I stripped bare and spilled out of my skin, my stories and my thinking overflowing. But she would never open up to me in the same way, she'd never divulge the intimacies of her relationship, she would never undress in front of me. Nor should she have had to, but I say this to show that as far as I was concerned there were no boundaries; they were a code I could not yet decipher. I am my mother's daughter. For my mother, the only boundary in life is a tangible object, like a fence or a line on the road. There is no other kind. A boundary as an abstract concept, between people, governing behaviour, with lines never to be crossed, is a foreign concept to her. No such line has ever constrained or contained my mother. For her, *everything* is for sharing—no matter the audience, no matter the subject. There is no filter.

Over time, years, my best friend began to withdraw. I sensed the distances between us, but still I ran full pelt towards her—I *needed* her to let me in. But she held firm and kept me at arm's length. It was exhausting, for both of us. I realise now that this was her way of establishing and reinforcing healthy, measured boundaries, something that I lacked the ability to do. I had thought that for a connection to be built, you had to omit boundaries.

Yet my best friend was still the one I went to when I needed someone in my corner, needed someone who could tell me that some broken things are not for mending, needed someone who would simply sit with me, in stillness, until I knew I'd be okay. And she was the person I went to, perhaps unfairly, when I was making the decision to end my marriage. There were many moments when I was a significant and unreasonable drain on her limited resources, but on a sweaty and stiflingly humid day in late February she was there for me. We met in the courtyard of the Lord Gladstone Hotel in Chippendale. I gently rocked myself and begged her to tell me what to do—and she told me that I already knew.

'I think you have been trying with incredible bravery to navigate a really complex situation. I have never known someone to so readily face their deepest challenges, and to be so open to being thrashed around by life in the process of the spirit of growing.'

I could imagine leaving my husband, but I couldn't imagine my life without her. But the life I could and could not imagine is the life I now live. I no longer have either of them.

Slowly, over time and then with distance after she returned to London, our lives fell out of sync. We were no longer living out of each other's pockets. There were missed calls that weren't returned, rambling voice notes that weren't replied to, lengthy texts that were read and then mislaid amongst the busyness of life. As much as she found her feelings at this time difficult to articulate, I couldn't talk about how I was feeling either. I was made to feel as if I were making something larger than it really was. She just seemed defensive. I was defensive too. I would apologise, *again*. I would put my feelings to the side, *again*. I began to dread our time together. Maybe we both did.

We all need to create an opportunity for our friendships to evolve. As Natasha Lunn writes in her book *Conversations on Love*, 'to sustain friendships—old and new—I think we have to learn to accept distance, and when to fight to repair it'. But after my divorce I found I had little to no fight left in me. I was worn out, I was tired.

As with my husband, my shared past with my best friend could be both incredibly beautiful and ridiculously frustrating. We struggled to allow each other space to develop and grow, clinging instead to the old versions of who we once were. As I continued to process my break-up, I needed her and my other friends to understand that I was not the same person I was last month, or last year. But it was an unrealistic and unfair expectation. It was up to me to tell her exactly who I was and what I needed from her. It's just that I was desperately afraid to—I was terrified of losing her.

Then one day she didn't answer another one of my calls, so I sent a text asking her how she was, and she replied saying that she'd had our friendship on her mind a lot recently, so she was sending an email with some thoughts. In her email she said she felt as though I wasn't telling her the truth anymore. That 'this feeling of not being able to be our true selves with each other is at odds with the label of best friend'. She wrote that for some 'that might just be a word, a term of endearment used pretty liberally', but that it was something she had always struggled with because she felt it implied 'all other friendships are less significant, but also because it puts pressure on a friendship to meet certain expectations'.

It's easy to feel pressured to remain a certain version of ourselves with friends we have known for substantial parts of our lives. I suppose that, as a result, I wasn't entirely honest with her. After my marriage breakdown, in re-establishing my independence I had created a separate person to love—myself.

I was in the thick of developing my sense of self, someone I could value, maintain and live with. I was no longer telling her every little thing I was thinking and feeling, as I had in the past, but that didn't necessarily mean I was withholding. Rather, it was a way of holding on to what little sense of self I did have. I had established a boundary, a healthy and measured boundary. And yes, the irony of her wanting me to reveal more of myself was not lost on me.

Our friendship faded. It wasn't as desperate or as terrifying as I had feared it would be. In fact, I felt . . . relief.

I removed the photos of her taken on our travels together from my walls. I boxed up the handmade cards and notes and gifts, along with those from my husband. The most brutal part of our friendship break-up were the notifications I received telling me that she had removed herself from our group chats, and then I realised she had not only unfollowed me but blocked me from her social media too. Her profile remains private, and I only hear occasional fragments about what she is up to from mutual friends.

When I look after others to my detriment, I fade. I disappear. She forced me to look at the kind of friend I am and the kind I want to be. She taught me to keep my sense of self, even when I want to be swept away by someone else's.

My psychologist told me that failure to fit in at an early age teaches us to develop a resilience that can ultimately help us flourish, and perhaps that is why I find I am now able to enter almost any sort of social setting with relative ease. But I wish I had known a decade ago, two decades ago even, that friends—real friends—love you for who you are, not only because you give them something.

Nobody ever really talks about the break-up of a friendship like they do a break-up with a partner, but it too is an immeasurable sorrow. Like my husband, my best friend has left an indelible mark on my life. She is embedded in so many of my memories. I often think of us in Paris, absorbing croissant after croissant, our cheeks full of remnants of butter. I think of us getting matching tattoos, indelible ink, of that flaky layered pastry—hers on her right arm and mine behind my left ear. Only now, I wish that I had not hidden mine away from myself. I wish I were able to see it—to think of her, to remember us.

My husband and my best friend were the heart and soul of my twenties, but I now found myself navigating my thirties without either of them.

I arrived at my new house, a terrace on Commodore Street, Newtown, an hour before the removalists, and I found myself standing in the bare bones of a strange place I was yet to call home. I was lonely, and desperately sad, and beset with uncertainty. I spent a whole hour pacing back and forth, wondering what I had done. Wondering if it had all been one huge mistake, wondering if I could still fix it. Maybe I should tell the removalist to turn the truck around and haul all my belongings back to the house I'd just left. My husband and I could arrange everything just as it had been before, and

I would tell him how sorry I was, and how silly this had all been—because surely things were never really *that* bad. I had once been happy; maybe I could still be happy. Surely the life I'd left behind, the life I knew, despite our many problems, was better than the unknown.

I wanted to pick up the phone and call him, to tell him I could not do this on my own. But I was brought back to the present by the *beep beep beep* of the removalist's truck reversing into my street. I had Mama's voice in my head telling me to trust myself, to trust my choices.

As each removalist box filed past me it confirmed what I already knew. I had done it. I had left my husband, and now I had to find a way to be okay without him.

I come from a long line of home cooks and feeders. We would eat when we were happy, we would eat when we were sad. But in the aftermath of my marriage, I found no joy in food. I found myself with no hunger, no appetite for cooking.

Even though the choice to leave was mine, I couldn't escape the stomach-churning sadness of our break-up.

The Oracle had explained to me that survival mode, fight-or-flight, is controlled by our sympathetic nervous system. *The accelerator.* It is our body's way of preparing us for and protecting us from potential threats, even though our bodies can't tell the difference between the threats that are minor and those that are major.

In order to be able to do its job properly, our brain needs to calm down, which is where our parasympathetic nervous system comes in. *The brake.* It lowers our blood pressure, promotes digestion and eliminates waste from our bodies—either by making us go to the toilet or, in my case, vomit. (This is my response to any extreme emotion. I vomit when I'm happy, when I'm sad, when I'm frightened and when I'm anxious.) It is the physical reaction to information that is so toxic or so exciting you simply must expel it. Our bodies respond immediately, releasing the distress as a coping mechanism.

In those early days in Newtown, the thought of food repulsed me. To avoid my feelings of nausea, I stopped eating. I think in some ways what I chose to eat (or not to eat) became the one and only thing I could control in an otherwise uncontrollable situation. My brain and my body became co-conspirators. I was on a hunger strike, not of my own volition.

At my saddest, I ate only boiled eggs.

Specifically hard-boiled eggs.

Just one per day.

I filled a small saucepan with cold water from the tap and placed it over a medium heat. I carefully lowered the free-range egg into the water, and when tiny bubbles formed I started the timer and let the egg simmer for eight minutes. When the timer sounded, I emptied the saucepan of water, leaving the egg lolling around the base of the saucepan. Lid on, I shook till the shell fully cracked. The egg, placed under running water and gently rubbed, shedded its shell to reveal a shock of white.

Those eggs nourished me when I couldn't nourish myself; they were the only thing that didn't make my stomach churn.

In order to eat properly again, I had to learn how to *rest-and-digest*. The more time we spend resting and digesting, the better our brains can distinguish regular life stresses from those that are life-threatening. I needed to work on how to manage my body and calm it. To understand how to feed myself emotionally.

But I wasn't there yet.

A week after I moved out, my cousin messaged me.

This might be nothing but one of my friends came across your husband on a dating app she's on. Just wanted to let you know in case you're not aware.

She sent me screenshots of his profile. It included photos he'd asked me to send him so that he would 'always be able to have photographs documenting our time together'.

The ground moved beneath me. Next thing I knew, I was on all fours, observing myself from the outside. I could see her but I did not recognise her. I could not comfort her.

My husband being on dating apps signified an ending, a betrayal that seared into my being. I didn't want us to be together, but I didn't want him *not* to want that. I didn't want him to be loved when I was so alone. I know how immature that sounds, but it's the truth.

Throughout our relationship, he made no secret of his desire to sleep with others. 'Am I not enough?' I'd ask. He couldn't—or *wouldn't*—see how humiliating it was, how it ate away at my sense of self, making me even more fearful of intimacy and more inhibited when it came to sex. And so, when I heard that he had begun to date so quickly, it exacerbated my greatest anxieties: that I was not deserving of him or his love. That I wasn't deserving of *anyone's* love.

I had a session with the Oracle in which I was an incoherent, blubbering mess.

'I just feel like I have taken ten steps backwards in terms of feeling outside of my body again and I can't sleep and I can't eat. I think there was just a big part of me that thought he would change, and I just feel really inadequate. I don't know what to do.'

She responded: 'As much as it hurts to watch someone who supposedly loved you throw away everything you had, so easily, you have to understand his behaviour is not about you anymore.'

I felt so small. So lost.

Being new to dating apps, my husband was surprised and appalled to discover that Sydney's online dating world was so very small, and he panicked. A flurry of desperate and remorseful calls, texts and FaceTime requests from him ensued. He was sorry I had found out in such a brutal way, he said, but he was also defensive, indignant in his belief that somehow *his* privacy had been invaded. I could barely respond and struggled to engage with him.

Shortly afterwards, I had to go back to the house we'd once shared to return my key and pick up a few last things. He wasn't home when I arrived, but he texted to say that I should go inside and get the last of my belongings.

I walked into 'our' bedroom, a space that should have been familiar, but found myself disorientated by the sight of a jumbo-sized box of condoms on the bedside table—as well as a discarded wrapper. At least he was finally getting laid, I thought to myself.

Nothing had changed between our first break-up and our marriage breakdown. But I couldn't help feeling like I was *owed* something. That even though he'd always made his desire to sleep with other people clear, he owed it to me (and to himself) to hold off, not to go and immediately seek the body of another. And as desperately selfish and hopeless as it might sound, I wanted him to show me he realised that doing so wouldn't make him feel happier. I honestly believed he wouldn't better himself by doing that. I think what hurt the most was my perception of his complete lack of self-awareness, his lack of a desire for growth, his inability to *see* and *work* on himself.

But the Guide had told us in no uncertain terms that we needed to disentangle our lives. That we were only responsible for ourselves now; that what we each chose to do was no longer any business of the other person. I had to realise my marriage was over; I was on my own. I couldn't demand that my husband work on himself; that was up to him. I had to focus on myself. As much as I tried not to obsess, I couldn't help wondering where he was, what he was doing and with whom. It was all-consuming; I felt numb and it affected my ability to function.

The Oracle was invaluable in her care, kindness and advice. She told me to practise coming into my own body, even in the middle of the night. It was a way to remind myself that I was here, that I was okay, that this pain would not last forever. She gave me a series of exercises to do: yawn, swallow and breathe deeply. Lay myself down in bed with a weighted blanket and tap my chest in a repeated rhythm. Move from the left to the right of my body and speak to my feet, legs, torso, arms, shoulders and face. Ask my body if it feels heavier or lighter, tighter or looser, warmer or colder. Tell my body to *feel*, to pull itself out of this state of numbness.

My friends rallied around me in the only way they could—from a distance, as Sydney had just entered its first Covid lockdown. Amelia would leave hampers of dark chocolate with sea salt, Sleepytime tea and jars full of melatonin on my doorstep. Robbie would sit on a stool outside on my porch and using gloves and tongs we would pass bottles of champagne between us through the front door. He would gaze into my puffy eyes and say lovingly: 'You have quite simply never looked worse.'

As I made it through yet another week, the daily ritual of hard-boiled eggs—topped with a drizzle of extra virgin olive oil and drowned in flakes of sea salt and freshly ground black pepper—gave way to the sunshine of runny soft-boiled eggs, served in an egg cup with toast soldiers dripping in butter.

So much of what I proceeded to eat throughout the weeks that followed came from my body feeding itself the things it needed most. I would go through cartons of free-range eggs each week—boiling them, scrambling them, making omelettes and Spanish tortillas. The weeks turned into months and I knew this period of introspection had to end, so I finally summoned the courage to tell Mama and Pa via FaceTime that I had left my marriage. I'd been holding off in the hope that Mama would emerge from her present episode, but it had gotten to a point where I couldn't wait any longer. Having to lie when they asked after him was only adding to my sense of untruthfulness. A lot of those initial conversations with Mum after I told her were disjointed, but what was beautiful was that my distress brought her back to herself. She knew that she was needed—that I needed her to get better.

While my mama couldn't be present with me in Sydney, I began to seek comfort in those few dishes she used to cook for me, expanding my diet beyond a thousand and one ways with eggs. I made her red lentil, white bean and ham hock soup. And almost every day I found myself in the kitchen making a single slice of grilled cheese on toast.

There were few things that I found more comforting than an open-faced grilled cheese sandwich. It was there at 3 am when I couldn't sleep, it was there at 8 am when I had my mum's voice in my head telling me to eat something even though I had no appetite, and it was there at 6 pm as something to look forward to, a reward for making it through another day.

For me, there was only one type of bread that would do: a fresh round loaf of uncut Sonoma miche, with its dark, blistered and caramelised crust. I pre-toasted the bread to ensure I didn't end up with a soggy bottom, topped it with enough sliced tasty cheddar cheese to cover every crevice and corner, then seasoned it generously with flakes of sea salt and freshly ground pepper. I placed it under the grill until the cheese was bubbling and golden. I sometimes added ham (which had to be leg ham off the bone) and thin slices of vine-ripened (but not too ripe) tomato, but that's as complicated as I got.

As the lockdown was extended week to week, my anxieties increased. Initially, I had been glad not to have to see people, to lick my wounds in private. But sustained isolation, and the uncertainty of the early days of the pandemic, made me feel raw. Even though I was still hardly eating, I distracted myself by cooking. Having a fridge full of food was one of the few things I could manage. Now that I had unrestricted access to my own money, I would spend hundreds of dollars ordering beautiful fresh produce and delicacies from Harris

Farm and meat from my gourmet ethical butcher, Feather and Bone. When the boxes arrived on my front step, I would spend an hour removing plastic, soaking and drying fruit and vegetables and wiping down items, in a Covid-cleansing ritual that verged on obsessive.

After weeks of barely leaving my strange new home, which still felt so foreign to me, I decided to stop myself fading into oblivion by attempting to connect with people. I thought of how my grandparents, who'd been farmers, would box up their surplus fruit, vegetables and eggs and give them to those who needed it, or mow their neighbours' lawns in exchange for freshly baked bread or golden roasted chickens. Inspired, I thought I would start cooking and give away the food I was making. I knocked on my neighbours' doors. Next door was Tracey, an academic at the nearby university who lived alone, working horrendously long hours on her latest research project. Then there was Harrie, a sole parent who had lost her job in the lockdown and quickly became one of my closest friends. Directly opposite were Jan and Sue, who were both essential workers. Sue worked in a drive-through Covid testing clinic while Jan was a midwife in the maternity ward of our local hospital. Beside them was Michael, a bloke who lived a rather solitary life and would disappear out bush with his swag at least once a month but whose booming voice I would occasionally hear outside my door bellowing a warm hello.

I introduced myself as someone who lived alone, loved to cook, and was going to be cooking *a lot*. 'I'm not going to poison you,' I said. 'Please let me cook for you.'

I hadn't come empty handed, either; I gave each household a box of freshly baked banana muffins (*not* Mama's store-bought ones). Some neighbours were brought to tears by the gesture; enforced isolation had made many people tender to the touch. I sensed how food and cooking nurtured feelings of community; being cooked for is such an intimate thing. Over the next six months, I perhaps took this concept too far, but through it all I came to know one truth—whether we are happy or sad, we must be fed.

While I was still eating simply, cooking was a different matter. I couldn't stop. I felt safe being back in the kitchen, especially when I stood there baking, covered in flour. It evoked memories of my mama. Those banana muffins I baked for my neighbours were the beginning of my feeding frenzy. I baked trays and trays of focaccia. I made curries, stews, stocks and soups, pasta sauces and rolls of cookie dough to stuff their freezers. If there is one thing I now know, it's that it's impossible to feel lonely when you bake for others, when you bake for those who will feel joy when they eat your food.

Eventually I found myself retrieving baking dishes from my neighbours every Saturday morning and returning to them later that day with homemade lasagne they could reheat that same night or freeze for later. Lasagne is something that must be prepared in advance. It is time-consuming, but far from difficult. I like to cook the meat sauce for at least six hours in my cast-iron pot. Often, I have it on low and slow for up to twenty-four hours. From the moment I begin sautéing the celery, carrot and onion in a bath of extra virgin olive oil, the whole house fills with the scent of a delicious promise. Lasagne-making is a ritualistic act for me. I find the entire process—from slowly stirring the sauce to rolling out and layering the pasta—grounding, restorative, meditative. You can make it and layer it and leave it to rest until the moment you are ready to bake it. Or, like I do, you can prepare it in what I like to call 'single lady portions' and freeze it to eat whenever you are craving a warm, cheesy cuddle.

It is not only cooking that grounds me. I am a bibliophile: I am obsessed with books. I adore the smell of them. I love how each book tells a story of having been caressed by a reader unknown to me, how that person's fingers have leafed through the pages, and, when interrupted, how they've folded the corner of the page—keeping their place but leaving a triangle-shaped crease, like a scar.

This meant that my job as a book publicist was more than just what I did for a living; it was a passion. I loved the air of expectation, anticipation, as a new book was launched into the world. I loved working with the authors who had invested so much of themselves into their books, from former prime ministers or directors of the FBI to bestselling children's authors and illustrators and retired cricket captains, from authors who wrote about giving no fucks or quitting sugar to entrepreneurs who had built up multimillion-dollar fitness empires.

As a publicist, I would accompany these authors on their promotional tours, visiting a different city each day, living out of a suitcase, managing events with thousands of attendees and corralling book-signing queues that might last for hours. I also had to cater to many different personality types: the extroverts who wanted someone to party with in the evenings, who never wanted to eat a meal alone; the introverts who needed peace and calm; the anxious first-time authors who needed support and reassurance. It's the kind of job in which you're so focused on meeting everyone's needs, it's easy to brush your own aside.

But that was fine. Losing myself in my work was something I *loved* to do. But then my marriage broke down, and hard on its heels came the first Covid lockdown, meaning I could no longer go to the office and all book tours were cancelled.

Until I found myself alone at home, I hadn't realised how much of my identity was tied up in my job and my marriage.

I'd had very little time for, or understanding of, myself and who I was without them. Living alone and working from home, no longer required me to be 'on' all the time, I recognised that I had never before had the time and space to discover who I was when I wasn't wearing the labels of 'wife' or 'publicist'. Now, though, there was no escaping it—or perhaps there was if I dared myself to believe it.

Bruised by the break-up with my husband, I wasn't interested in looking in the mirror but I wanted validation from others. As Jessie Tu wrote in her novel *A Lonely Girl Is a Dangerous Thing*: 'The hunger rises when things start to settle. And then I crave the attention of men. It feels more powerful to be desired than to desire. There's safety in being wanted. No risk in being desired.'

This was not necessarily the best mindset with which to enter the world of online dating, but when the first lockdown lifted in June 2020 I did so anyway, and—ever the overachiever—I did so with dogged determination, approaching it methodically and strategically. I did my research thoroughly. As a first timer, I didn't discriminate. I was a woman determined to be visible from every angle, signing up to Bumble, Tinder, Hinge and even eharmony (though my time on the latter was short-lived).

The apps became all-consuming. I cannot tell you the sheer number of hours I spent overthinking EVERY. SINGLE. THING. Agonising over my selection of pictures or the order in which they appeared. Swiping left, and right, and left again. I spent hours debating who should make the first move and, if I made it, what I should say, how I could present myself as the perfect balance between interested and interesting.

Three months after separating from my husband, and two months after his first foray into online dating, I had my own first date, with an Italian from Bumble. As he approached my front door, my first thought was that he was a *lot* shorter than his profile pictures had led me to believe, but he was dressed beautifully in monotone layers of linen and had a perfectly manicured moustache. (I am such a sucker for facial hair.)

Together we rolled out egg pasta dough into thin, almost transparent, lasagne sheets and layered them with a ragù that I'd had simmering for the past twenty-four hours— the very same ragù my husband had taught me to make on our second date. It was ambitious to make an iconic Italian dish for someone of Italian heritage, but I was determined to impress. And if I say so myself, the lasagne was perfection. The crispy mozzarella topping gave way to soft pillowy layers of bechamel, and the meat sauce had the kind of depth and richness that can only be achieved after hours on the stove. Two slices in and he still wanted more—so much so, he insisted on returning to the kitchen at 2 am to have one last mouthful before he headed home.

For our second date, I treated myself to a crisp new white wrap dress that hugged my hips and showcased my cleavage. When I left the house to show Harrie what I was wearing— running high on nerves and adrenaline—the door slammed shut behind me and I realised I had locked myself out mere moments before the Italian was due to arrive. The benefit of having spent the past few months feeding my neighbours was that they all rallied around in my hour of need. Michael, who lived directly opposite, came to the rescue in his fluoro workwear. Carrying a ladder through Tracey's house to her back yard, he proceeded to climb nimbly over the fence separating her place from mine, letting himself in through my back door and opening the front door to me just in time. I do wonder what the Italian must have thought when he arrived to find all my neighbours loitering out the front, waiting for a glimpse of him.

I ushered him inside to the kitchen, where he taught me how to make buttery, creamy carbonara, just like his nonna had taught him. It is such a beautifully simple dish—requiring nothing more than eggs, guanciale and parmesan (without a dash of cream in sight)—and as I sat on the kitchen bench, trying to make conversation in my high school Italian, I thought how nice it was to be cooked for again.

I told the Italian *in* Italian that I would make my own tiramisu. It was his turn to be the observer as I whisked the egg yolks with sugar and vanilla until the mixture was thick and pale. I folded in the mascarpone, resisting the urge to scoop up the creamy batter and eat it by the handful, straight from the mixing bowl. But then I relented, sliding two fingers along the inside of the bowl and into my mouth. In a separate bowl, the egg whites were combined with sugar, one spoonful at a time, and now I was an alchemist, whipping up a glossy, stiff meringue. The layering of a tiramisu, like the layering of a lasagne, is therapeutic. Bathing the savoiardi biscuits in freshly brewed coffee is perhaps my favourite part.

I looked up, checking to see if the Italian was anticipating the treat as much as I was, to find that he had produced his laptop and was setting it up on the kitchen bench. Indifferent to the tiramisu I was making, he asked me to proofread a tender submission. Two hours in and the date had become little more than a work meeting. I felt used, and made no effort to hide my annoyance. I drank wine, lots of it. Eventually, with him too intoxicated to drive home and me too intoxicated to think to ask him to take an Uber, we stumbled up to bed. I'd had no thoughts of intimacy, but I woke some time later to the uncomfortable sensation of him inserting his fingers into me. He asked me why I wasn't more excited. The thing is, I told him, being awake is a fundamental precursor to arousal and consent. My sobriety was swiftly regained and I asked him to leave. If he couldn't drive, he could walk.

The date wasn't a complete loss, though, as I wrote in my journal:

> *I am beginning to find my voice. The ability and power to say no.*
>   *To **stop** sex if I do NOT want to have it.*

And tiramisu, I discovered, is even more magnificent the following day, especially when eaten with the pleasure of your own company.

My next date was with an artist. We matched on Bumble and agreed to go for a walk. He was thirty-seven, Swiss, and ridiculously good-looking. Amelia nicknamed him the Lindt Ball. We met late on a Sunday afternoon. I was wearing white Veja sneakers and a gingham dress that wrapped tightly around my body. He texted me to say he had arrived at my house, but when I opened the door he wasn't there. Not entirely convinced that this wasn't one of those mortifying scenarios I had read about in which your date stands you up and films your reaction, I stepped onto the street to find him hidden by a banana palm, beaming at me.

We began walking around Sydney Park, and he was so tall I had to strain my neck to look up at him. Skipping the small talk, we spoke of our childhoods, about the unrealistic expectations we placed both on ourselves and on our relationships, and about the ways in which our lives hadn't quite turned out as we had hoped, agreeing that we were here for the unexpected surprises anyway. We returned to my house, completely engrossed in each other and conversation, and drank multiple cups of tea. I could have spent hours more with him, suspended in time and longing, if we hadn't been interrupted by Rob, whom I had almost forgotten I was having dinner with. Rob declared the Lindt Ball to be one of the most attractive men he had ever seen, which meant a lot coming from him; he had known many beautiful men.

The Lindt Ball texted me almost immediately after I had hugged him goodbye, asking to see me again, and suggesting another walk and dinner the very next day. When you are in the mindfuck that is dating in the modern world, little things that wouldn't normally register are given far too much weight. His text made no promises, conveyed no romantic expectation but it still made me feel ridiculously happy. I made myself a cup of hot tea and it felt like a warm kiss on my lips.

He arrived at my house the next day with his biceps bulging from a tight light grey cotton tee, carrying a jar filled with a curated selection of T2 tea. Inside its perfumed glass lay perhaps the best gift he could have given me—French Earl Grey. He was carrying a vintage film camera, which he used to take photos of me as I proceeded to make us dinner. The main course was chicken meatballs, which have a beautiful lightness to them as they are boiled in stock rather than fried in oil. They're then served in a tender tomato and zesty lemon broth with a drizzle of olive oil and shavings of parmesan. For dessert, I made a towering carrot cake layered with generous lashings of cream cheese icing. We talked nonstop, stifling our yawns as the late night gave way to early morning.

We began to see each other frequently; at one point I had seen him four times in five days. It was intense, but it was so lovely to feel seen by someone again. I texted him, suggesting dishes we might make together for our next dinner date, and he replied:

Charlotte, you've already impressed me. Being with you is impressive. You don't have to do any more than be you.

Nobody had ever said that to me before. In my journal I wrote:

I feel like I am showing love through food! Making love through food.

It was a rainy Friday and I was busy planning a feast for the Lindt Ball that evening. I went to my fishmonger first thing in the morning and bought fresh kingfish, salmon and tuna sashimi for our entree, and some beautiful salmon fillets with which I planned to make baked pasta parcels with a dash of cream, green peas and parsley for our main. On my lunch break, I made my lemon olive oil cake for dessert.

The evening was perfect. We ate and talked nonstop (and sober, mind you) until 3 am. But I cringe as I recall what happened next. When he rose to leave, I rose too, and leaned in to kiss him. And he rejected me. It was awkward—hilariously so. As the sky wept, I couldn't help but laugh, and cringe, and laugh again.

The next morning, I sipped from my mug of freshly brewed tea and wrote him a text apologising for making him feel uncomfortable. He replied that I was a beautiful woman and a kiss from me hadn't made him 'uncomfortable', but he wanted to ensure he was ready to be the best version of himself in something more than a friendship.

The Lindt Ball might not have been ready, but I was. I wrote in my journal:

> *It's so scary for me to feel this drawn, connected and attracted to someone. To feel this alive.*
>
> *It's scary because it's such a new feeling.*
>
> *Because for so long in my marriage I didn't feel any of those things. I was just surviving. I was clinging on to something that was broken for so long that I stifled any sense of what I wanted.*

I knew what I wanted: I wanted intimacy. I wanted to get to know him more deeply, to soak him up. To breathe him in. The Oracle's advice was, as always, invaluable. Wallow in these long conversations and shared moments, she advised.

Be vulnerable. Be inquisitive. Articulate desires. Constantly check in on what it is that you are needing and wanting.

I needed affection, I wanted touch; I'd been grieving the loss of those things with my husband, and I was craving them from the Lindt Ball.

His birthday came around, and we spent the cold dreary day holed up in my house together making ricotta gnocchi in a sweet tomato and basil sauce. I had spent hours labouring over his birthday cake before he arrived, and for the first time in my life I made the most perfect chiffon. It was at least fifteen centimetres in height and so ridiculously light and fluffy it was as though it were made of air. I dusted it with icing sugar and served it with a thick dollop of cream and a jar of fragrant, moscato-infused peaches. I will forever remember the look of pure surprise and delight that spread across his face as he took his first mouthful. 'You have ruined food for me,' he said to me on leaving. 'I can't wait to eat with you again.'

He was telling me he loved my food, but I felt as though he was saying he was falling in love with *me*.

On one of our last dates, we ventured into that hotbed of the Covid-era social scene, Bunnings, where we acquired everything this gorgeous European needed (including outrageously overpriced firewood) to teach me how to light a fire the Swiss way. We sat on cushions on the floor of my living room and watched the flames burn brightly, and I longed to kiss him, but after what had happened on my last attempt, I didn't dare.

Finally, after many weeks and walks and dinners and copious amounts of mixed messages, I found myself sitting alone in front of the fire one night and, with the help of some liquid courage, I sent him a message telling him how desperately I wanted to kiss him.

He responded saying that my message had come as a surprise.

> I know we met on Bumble, but I've taken from our friendship a sense of happiness and excitement that has made me realise who and what I can be for myself. This version of me is infinitely better than the person I seem to become in a relationship, and I know that this sounds selfish, but I want to live like this for a while and focus on interactions that are different from the ones I'd have with a partner.

I was angry. Angry at myself. Angry because I had let myself get swept up in the *idea* of him. I was also angry that while he wasn't interested in me romantically, he loved how much better I made him feel about himself. I hated that. I'd spent far too long propping up a man's ego in my marriage.

I texted him back:

> I'm not here to make someone better for someone else.
> I spent nine years doing that already. This isn't to say that
> I don't want to be friends with you moving forward, but
> for me a relationship that is only a friendship is different.
> It's simply a different level of investment from me.
>
> I can't cook for you anymore.

I went back online and had my first, and only, date from Hinge. Though he was nice, extremely fit and ridiculously clean (almost too clean), it was no Elizabeth Day–style, meet-your-future-husband-on-Hinge love story. I made barramundi baked in parcels with soy, mirin and ginger sauce on a bed of Asian greens, but he refused to eat the bok choy, saying it was too slimy. We had a drunkenly awkward attempt at sex but he couldn't maintain an erection. I told him I was tired anyway, that I would rather just cuddle and go to sleep. 'Don't try to make this about you,' he replied.

Next was a date with the Van-lifer, a hairy nomad with kind green eyes who arrived at my house carrying a case of beer. The whole case wasn't intended for me, though, thank goodness, something he made clear from the get-go. He was taking everything but a six pack to his mate's later that evening. I couldn't understand him and he couldn't understand me; it wasn't that he spoke another language, it was just that he used a kind of slang I just couldn't grasp. We consumed one beer each before realising we weren't quite a match, so it was back to his van he went, beer in tow. He texted me to say how lovely it was to meet me and wished me well.

There were the men who came and went, and came again. They gave me false hope, and just enough of a sense of misplaced optimism that I allowed myself to think maybe *this* was it. Maybe *he* was the one. Somehow they seemed to know when a woman was stuck in the 'in-between', at her most vulnerable and most lonesome—and then there they were. Well, there was Camo Pants anyway, with his charm and his good looks. In his mid-thirties, he ran a successful building project management business that took him up and down the east coast.

We met on Bumble. He had one of those profiles in which he looked so vastly different in each photo I couldn't quite grasp which version of him was the *real* one. He didn't have an Instagram or Facebook account, but he did have an architecturally designed, award-winning house. This was appealing to me; I'd spent far too much of my youth designing and building houses for *The Sims*. He sent me photographs and a link to the architect's blog about the building and design process. I could see myself inside that house, could imagine making a Sunday roast with all the trimmings in that kitchen, cooking for him. I just wanted to be someone's *someone*. To have a home.

I call him Camo Pants because that's what he wore on our first date. He did have the courtesy to warn me of the fact— *FYI slippers are on and the only pants I could find that aren't work related are camo*—but I think I was so distracted by having almost forgotten I was due to run an online baking class for Dymocks Books that same night that opening the door to the vision of his grey camo cargo pants still took me by surprise. As soon as he arrived, I thrust a glass of wine in his hand and retreated to the kitchen, where my computer and an out-of-body experience were waiting.

Looking back, my whole house could have been pillaged by this complete stranger while I was preoccupied working. But he sat there and watched, and he even laughed when my mum continuously interrupted the live demonstration with multiple texts and phone calls to tell me: 'Charli, Aunty Paula told me you're supposed to be cooking. Did you remember?' Well, no, Mama. I was actually supposed to be on a date.

On finishing my event, I found him reading Rupi Kaur's *Milk and Honey* on my couch, his wineglass now empty. The date, once we finally started it, was fabulous. One of those brilliant nights of chemistry and cheek and sass and spontaneity that I had been craving. We sat on my kitchen steps and ate tomatoey, garlicky, oily spaghetti vongole by the bowlful, guzzled far too much crisp white wine and devoured the still-warm honey madeleines I had baked over Zoom earlier in the evening. Armed with a belly full of booze and the new fire-starting skills I had acquired from the Lindt Ball, I lit a raging fire in what I would soon come to realise was my basically ornamental fireplace. We stretched out on a blanket in front of it and had the passionate kiss I had been craving during those weeks spent unsuccessfully wooing the Swiss. A kiss that was all-consuming—so much so, it took us a minute too long to realise that the fire had taken over the fireplace and risen up the chimney—both internally and externally.

That was the last fire I lit at Commodore Street, but it wasn't the last time I saw Camo Pants. He became my spontaneous fuck buddy, a last-minute booty call whenever he happened to roll into town. Camo Pants, I came to realise, had an address book full of women along the east coast whom he could approach for, well, accommodation. I don't know why I allowed myself to join his list of homestays so willingly. Though he was a bloody brilliant kisser, it isn't as though he treated me nicely or showed any real interest in me. He never even gave me an orgasm. He would rarely bring anything with him, just walk straight through the door and into the shower. He would eat my food and drink my wine, have sex with me and then fall into a deep sleep on the furthest side of the bed. He would be up and out of the house by 5 am, sometimes with breakfast (his favourite being avocado and Vegemite on sourdough toast), sometimes without. There were never any follow-up texts, no expressions of gratitude, and I would be left, a lady-in-waiting. Wallowing in wanting.

There was never a major falling out between us, no final farewell; things just sort of . . . *fizzled*. He'd still pop up in my inbox from time to time, to touch base, like when he saw my house appear on a design website or when he just so happened to be in my neighbourhood. Really, though, I think he was just looking for any excuse to send a dick pic—or video, as he did most recently. It was artistic, at least. Black and white, the video pans from a creek to an outdoor shower, water flowing, and he reveals himself from the neck down—hairy, toned, wet, erect—his image reflected in a small round mirror hanging from the shower head. He, unlike me, never had any problem articulating exactly what he wanted.

He helped me realise the problem with the kind of man I was attracted to and the traits I was manifesting in a partner—someone who was successful, someone who was ambitious. Success and ambition were such driving forces for these men that they did not want to, or simply could not, prioritise a relationship.

I look back now on those months of online dating as a phase of self-sabotage. I responded to matches indiscriminately. Spontaneous dates turned into spontaneous one-night stands. And not the fun kind either. I'm talking about men who, on meeting, I was not the slightest bit attracted to—nor they to me, probably. So, I drank enough alcohol to find the jokes funny, to find the mundane banter somehow charming, to find the uninteresting interesting, and then we would sleep together. Perhaps I thought by being close to someone, anyone, for just one night, the intense ache of loneliness might ease just a little.

I had the occasional one-night stand that didn't even involve a meal first. For some this would be routine but for me, it was something that left me questioning my decision-making and my sense of self-worth. I'd meet up with men I had matched with on multiple dating platforms and have fantastic, engaging conversations of goosebump-inducing intimacy, in which I allowed myself to unfurl, only to wake the next day to discover my bed was empty and they'd deleted our chat history or deleted their profiles entirely.

I fret, I fret, I fret.

I'm not sure why I decided to make contact with my father for the first time in almost five years. Maybe it was a by-product of being in extended isolation where I had more time to think, to become cognisant of my absent father. We met at my favourite local coffee shop. He was wearing a black knitted jumper, Birkenstocks with socks and a satchel slung over his right shoulder. His beard was still full, but now it was grey. He had gotten older. Looking at him was disorientating. It was like looking at a male version of myself in the mirror; our oval faces and large eyes and long lashes were nearly identical.

I was starving but only ordered a pot of tea, even ordering tea was anxiety-inducing. All I wanted was French Earl Grey but they only had English breakfast. I was irritable, unsettled, off-kilter. He was just as I remembered: distant, and appeared only mildly interested in my life. When I told him about my separation, he responded by saying that my husband had never liked him anyway—this was not true, but I said nothing. When I told him that I was working on another book idea, he was surprised. He didn't even know that I had published a first. I then realised that he had not been thinking of me, that he had not been following me or my life, even on social media. That he had no idea who I was. And I, for my part, did not know this man in front of me. Guarded, I had no idea what to say to him. Apart from our genes, we had virtually nothing in common. There was nothing that bound us together, aside from my beautiful siblings. But just as I had learned with my husband, I knew I could not force my father to be the man I longed for him to be.

I know now that having an absent father doesn't necessarily imply there will be a return. I think of him not as a father who left but a father who faded. Once so present, so vibrant, he had since retreated to a place where I could not reach him, leaving me with a sense of rejection and worthlessness. If only my father, a decade before, had said that he wasn't coping, that he needed time, space, it would have been hard to accept but I would have understood. It would have made his leaving me so much *easier*.

FADE

If only the men in my life had been brave enough to open up to me about their vulnerabilities, then I would have understood that the challenges were with *them*, not me. Instead, I made their shortcomings my own; I interpreted their self-absorption as confirmation of my deep-seated belief that I was not good enough, that I wasn't worthy of a man's love. After all, I didn't even have the love of my father.

But growing up I was loved. I knew that then and I still know it now, for paternal love comes in many forms. And I was blessed to find a father in Pa. For his unconditional love, I am eternally grateful.

Seeing my father again after all those years exacerbated my intense desire for validation, rather than easing it. So, as a distraction, I threw myself back into dating. I met the Rower on Bumble. He asked me when I was free for a drink.

'Do you want to come over and I'll cook dinner?' I replied.

'How could I possibly refuse?' he said.

He arrived wearing a ribbed, army-green woollen jumper, black jeans and rugged R.M. Williams. He had a boyishly charming mop of dark brown hair that he had to keep sweeping away from his eyes. I could tell he was incredibly shy, that he found it hard to communicate, but there was a mysterious confidence to him that had me intrigued—or perhaps I found his aloofness a challenge that I had to conquer.

Our first date was essentially platonic. It's not that I wasn't attracted to him, or interested in seeing him again; I was just left feeling indifferent. I was so exhausted by the months of rejection and dejection that had led up to our meeting that I was no longer willing to allow myself to invest in someone else too quickly or easily.

Our second date took place the night after I'd hosted a friend's thirtieth birthday party and I found myself with an unexpected stowaway—my friend Ali—staying in my spare bedroom. I messaged the Rower with a heads-up and an offer to reschedule, but he replied that he would bring enough steaks for all of us. I was exhausted and hungover from the all-night party, and Ali couldn't believe I was going ahead with the date.

The Rower arrived with some of the most beautiful eye fillet steaks I had ever seen and a bottle of cab sav, which we opened immediately to ease the tension of this unexpected group date.

Ali made a moreish chargrilled broccoli salad with chickpeas while the Rower and I ventured outside, and he taught me how to barbecue a steak. He held my hand in his and showed me how to test if a steak was done. Pressing the index finger and thumb of one of my hands together, and then using the index finger of my other hand to touch the fleshy area under my thumb, he told me that this was what a rare steak felt like to touch. By pressing my middle finger and thumb together and touching the area beneath my thumb, I could see what medium–rare felt like. Medium to medium–well could be gauged by touching my ring finger and thumb together, well-done my pinky and thumb. It was a cooking hack I had never heard before and one I have never forgotten. We seared the steaks, with the Rower achieving the perfect crisscross grill marks on each fillet, and then removed them to rest. The dinner was a bit of a blur, thanks to my fog of nerves, but I can distinctly remember that Ali's valiant attempts to engage the Rower in conversation were gruelling and she turned to the open bottle of wine for inspiration.

When we'd finished eating, Ali excused herself and headed to bed. Giggling nervously at the situation I found myself in, and with my fear of rejection still riding high after my experience with the Lindt Ball, I somehow worked up the courage to invite the Rower to stay over. We undressed, keeping our backs to each other respectfully. But then I just thought, *fuck it*, and I walked over to his side of the bed in my new set of lingerie and kissed him.

It was slow, tentative and awkward at first. Our front teeth accidentally collided, we weren't quite sure where to put our hands, but then, as if I were as light as a feather, he lifted me onto my bed, and for the next five hours we fooled around between my linen sheets—ever so quietly, for fear of Ali hearing us. He told me that I challenged and excited him, and I guess he challenged and excited me, too.

I texted him in the morning, thanking him for coming over, explaining how absolutely shattered I felt after a sleepless night of overstimulation and apologising for not having made a move sooner. He replied:

> I could be a little more forward next time and I'm more comfortable with you now so it's as much my fault.

We began to see each other regularly, usually once during the working week and then again on the weekend. Our dates were mostly planned at the last minute and he rarely committed to a set time; he would just rock up at my house when he felt like it. With Sydney nightlife back in full swing after the recent lockdown, we began visiting some of my favourite local restaurants. I quickly realised that this rower of mine had a lot of dietary restrictions, which I now understand were a form of control for him, driven by issues he had with his body, so our

FADE

meals tended to revolve around meat. We'd devour beef tartare with fried onions, or black Angus steak frites with sauce Diane and a bottle of gamay at Cafe Paci. We would roll out of LP's Quality Meats bloated by the blood sausage, charcuterie and aged rib eye. Continental Deli became our regular haunt; seated at the bar we'd each order their steak tartare, served with freshly shaved parmesan and gaufrette potato chips, and wash it down with dirty martinis.

As we spent more time together and he gradually revealed more of himself, our sex became increasingly complicated and our intimacy infrequent. We stopped kissing almost entirely and I felt like a life force had been taken away from me; I'd always found kissing to be the ultimate form of affection. He didn't willingly divulge any information and I didn't ask any questions. I wasn't sure what to say, where to start. But for some reason, I felt as though I could do for him what nobody has been able to do for me—I thought I could help him, I could rescue him.

The sex was just one major issue between us, and I tried to stifle the knowledge that he and I were incompatible in an immense number of ways and that this relationship was not going to work. Instead, I continued to push myself out of my comfort zone and, in a futile attempt to better understand him, I *dived* headfirst into his world in the most literal sense, bursting from my inner-city bubble and heading to the northern beaches.

It was a gloriously sunny Sunday. I had lost so much weight that I could fit comfortably into a pair of jeans that would have previously prevented me from breathing. I took the ferry to Manly, and he met me in his giant four-wheel drive. It was so big that I needed his help to clamber into the passenger seat, and it was so loud I could barely hear myself think. He drove us to Manly Dam, where he suggested we go for a walk.

If there is one thing you should know about me, it is that I do not hike, thanks to a significant amount of unprocessed trauma from a horrific week-long Outward Bound experience when I was fifteen, where I was forced to eat SPAM and scroggin (a mixture of nuts, carob and desiccated coconut) and developed lifelong physical and mental scars from thigh chafing. The jeans I was now wearing were most certainly not designed for hiking, and with a sinking feeling I realised that chafing was inevitable. But ever the people-pleaser, I agreed that a walk would be lovely, and thus we began a relentless three-hour, seven-kilometre hike. We spent hours walking in almost complete silence. I was sweating. I was sunburned. I was losing the will to live with every step. But of course, I didn't tell him as much.

The following weekend he drove me to North Head, where a panoramic view of Sydney Harbour and the city's skyline awaited us, to watch the sun set. There he opened the boot of his car to reveal a picnic basket overflowing with Ortiz anchovies, stuffed peppers, Sicilian olives, freshly baked baguettes, creamy mozzarella, nutty jamón ibérico and a bottle of shiraz covered in dust from his cellar. I had never been taken out on a picnic before; it felt romantic. He lifted me up and kissed me. We ate the feast he had prepared. I felt happy.

Not long after that, in late August, he invited me to his house for the weekend. It was the first time I'd been invited to a sleepover at the house of a man—who wasn't my husband. He was vague when I asked what I should bring (other than snake-proof activewear, so that we could go on a hike through the national park—*great*), so I went ahead and packed all the wrong things, including my hairdryer and straightener. I took the bus from Wynyard to the beachside suburb of Mona Vale, where he picked me up, and we drove to Pittwater. We crossed the choppy water in his tiny tinnie and tied up at the dock attached to his home.

He told me that he hadn't had anyone over in more than a year. I felt special, chosen. He showed me his studio and took me through his sketchbooks, which were filled with drawings of the rich landscape and abundant bush that surrounded his home. He brought out his guitar and sang to me. Then we changed into our walking gear and embarked on a four-hour hike through the bush, sighting just one brown snake. He deemed this the perfect time to tell me that they didn't keep antivenom in the remote area where he lived, and I remembered it was a boat and car ride to the nearest hospital. We returned to his house, washed the day away (removing a few bloodthirsty leeches I had acquired) and took a bottle of wine to the water's edge, where we watched the sun set. I allowed myself to feel at home somewhere, and with someone, completely foreign to me. But I suppose I have sometimes felt like a foreigner in my own body, too.

As we talked, the Rower became increasingly vulnerable, but I realised that he was hating himself for it. Soon, the shutters came down and he retreated into himself. I felt as though he wished I was no longer there—or perhaps that was a feeling I projected onto him—and the rest of the night was so uncomfortable. Almost unbearable.

We woke early. I was packing my things, preparing to make the long journey home, when some of his friends stopped by and invited the two of us to their weekly Sunday night dinner. There was a part of me that wanted to stay, to take a step further into his world, but I could tell he was willing me to say no, so I politely declined. I wrote in my journal that night:

Why? Why am I so desperate to be loved? So desperate to be understood?

I didn't see him again until mid-September, when we'd planned a weekend away to visit Amelia and her then partner in Orange. Of all my friends, they were the ones I felt most comfortable introducing this shy, reclusive man to, as they were all from the Northern Beaches and surely would find some things in common.

We arrived in the dark. The Rower and Amelia's boyfriend bonded over barbecuing eye fillet steaks while Amelia and I made a creamy layered potato bake and a bitter leafy green salad. We drank countless bottles of local wine. The Rower was so drunk that when he went to retrieve his bag from his car he tripped and fell, hurting himself. He was embarrassed.

The next day we were due to make back-to-back winery visits, and he was so hungover that as the day passed he grew more and more silent and became increasingly distant. We visited Tamburlaine, Angullong and Hoosegg, and finished at Stockman's Ridge, sampling wines until we were once again drunk. I begged the Rower to talk to me, to let me in. But he dismissed me. The rest of the night is a haze, but I know I accidentally broke my friends' beloved La-Z-Boy recliner and found myself retreating to bed alone, my tail between my legs. I woke in the middle of the night and reached for him but he brushed me off. I drunkenly sobbed into his back but he refused to indulge me any further, telling me that he needed to sleep as we had a long drive in the morning.

Driving home, I once again pressed him to talk to me.

He said that he knew I could tell something was happening for him at that moment, but he refused to talk about it. I needed a depth of communication that he would never be able to give me. He had erected walls around himself that I wouldn't be able to breach.

He pulled up outside my house and helped me carry my things in from the car. His birthday was coming up later that week, but he was noncommittal when we spoke of plans, and there was a part of me that knew this would be the last time I saw him. I was hungry, tired and teary. He ghosted me after that weekend away in Orange, and even though the silence was deafening, I still sent one last text.

> I am not really sure what's going on for you at the moment but I know you've made it clear you don't want to talk about it, and that's absolutely fine. Communication is really important to me and I don't at all like being kept at a distance. I really do wish you all the best but I can't do this anymore.

He never replied.

The Oracle called me a 'shame vacuum'. She told me that I couldn't keep carrying people's shame. I couldn't keep believing that I could rescue them. At first I thought the Rower didn't want or need to be rescued—well, not by me anyway. Then I realised: you can't rescue someone when you're in need of rescuing yourself.

I have always adored the female body, in all its various shapes and sizes. Growing up in a family of voluptuous body-positive women made sure of that. Stretch marks, sagging breasts, pubic hair—even female facial hair—were all normalised. My mother will proudly tell anyone who cares to listen that she has never shaved, plucked or waxed. I've never felt any embarrassment at seeing my grandmother or my mother or my friends naked, or them seeing me the same way. But it wasn't until I met the Couple that I had ever been with a woman intimately.

I matched with them on Tinder. They were incredibly intelligent and creative, charming, and obscenely good-looking. She led the charge.

> We usually chat to people together, but also he basically doesn't use his phone or social media so I do more.

I replied:

> I like a woman who takes charge.

(And then immediately regretted it.)

The fact is, I was curious. I wanted to understand how a couple could navigate what I could never accept in my husband—his desire to sleep with other people—and how they managed to do it without fracturing.

She asked me if I had ever been with a woman before. I told her I hadn't. It turned out she hadn't either until a year before. The Couple had been together for three years and had talked about being open to sharing sexual experiences with others from day one.

> It's been fun, weird, sexy and at times uncomfortable (as is life!) but ultimately great for us. We're pretty open and relaxed about it all, which helps, I think.

I texted her about books, crying into pasta with friends, organic wine, restaurant openings, restaurant closings and eating whole tins of Ortiz anchovies by myself. She replied:

> Is it weird how much that endears you to me?

We took a break from texting, opting to save the getting-to-know-you until her partner returned from a business trip and we could meet in person.

There were a few false starts before that happened. Rob went through a break-up and I cancelled a date with the Couple to spend the night cooking for him. The Couple double-booked me. One of them got sick. I got cold feet. She texted me:

> Hey, just wanted to add there's absolutely no pressure here, we think it would be cool to meet for a drink because you seem great but please don't feel you're committing to doing anything other than meeting and

chatting. We're very relaxed and like to communicate openly throughout everything.

We finally agreed to meet the following Saturday at Lobo Plantation, a rum bar I had never been to before. Saturday rolled around and I was surprisingly calm, I think because I was genuinely just treating it as a meet and greet, to see what sense we got of each other, with the option to then plan a second meeting from there.

I arrived at Lobo Plantation right on time and stumbled upon them fumbling with the QR code at check-in. We hugged warmly and headed down the curved staircase. I immediately felt as though I had been transported to the streets of Havana with the bar's rattan chairs, kitsch cocktails, banana palms and crumbling patina.

We slipped into the only available red booth and ordered spiced rum cocktails. A lot of them. I felt like I was on a night out with old friends. Bar snacks arrived—spicy little empanada pillows that you could devour in two bites, barely enough to soak up the rum. She excused herself to go to the bathroom, and he and I were left alone. He was gorgeous and I found there was a part of me that wished it was just the two of us on the date. Maybe she wouldn't come back, I thought hopefully.

She did.

Then he went to the bathroom and she and I were left alone. I realised then that this was a test, that they were both attempting to gauge my interest and enthusiasm, and so I leaned into them. I flirted with adventure and possibility. I left for the bathroom when he returned, giving them time to discuss if they wanted to pursue anything, and when I sat back at the table they invited me back to their house in Bondi. Clearly, I had met with their approval. I momentarily considered their offer, but decided I would feel more comfortable taking them to my house.

We jumped in an Uber, me in the front and the two of them in the back, and on the way to Commodore Street I remembered the vodka pasta sauce I had made earlier in the day in preparation for my solo, perhaps drunken, return home and volunteered to make them dinner.

We opened a bottle of red wine, and I cooked rigatoni in boiling salted water. I ladled the vodka sauce onto the pasta and covered it in freshly grated parmesan. We ate—flirting, touching, drinking—until anticipation made me impatient. We moved from the dining table to the couch, with her in the middle. She encouraged him and me to lean across her and kiss, while she watched. I could feel the warmth of her breath on my cheek. Then she kissed me.

We peeled ourselves from the couch and moved upstairs to my bedroom, where we took it in turns to watch each other undress. She had the body of a pin-up, a perfect hourglass with the tiniest pinch of a waist. His body was beautiful, too. Toned, hairless, smooth. They had some rules. No penetrative sex with the third was one of these: sucking, yes, but no fucking.

For a long time, I have been so in my head when it came to oral sex that I couldn't be in my body. I would be overwhelmed with worry about how I tasted, my scent, what I looked like from that angle, how long it would take me to orgasm—that is, if I could orgasm, and didn't have to fake it to make my spiralling anxiety stop. But oddly, as amateurish as I felt, or as inept as I may have been, having a woman show me and respond to me made me finally able to appreciate all of my own body as well.

After, I sat on the edge of my bed and watched the two of them make love between my lavender linen sheets. They weren't looking at each other, though; they were looking at me. As someone who had never even watched soft porn, I found this fascinating. He pulled away from her and came towards me and kissed me passionately. I felt desired. I was relearning that sex is also about play. I am not sure if this was what did it, but something seemed to shift for her. She no longer seemed at ease. She was no longer comfortable or curious. She wanted to leave, and quickly.

I put on my nightgown as they hurriedly got dressed. I walked them to the door and watched them run into the night.

Stripping off my nightgown, I stepped into the shower, and as the steaming-hot water poured over me I began to feel that the night had been a gift, for me at least. After my marriage ended, I was left wondering how a couple—no matter how confident and comfortable they are in their relationship—adjusts to an open relationship, adjusts to the unknown addition of a third. How could they predict what that person, or that experience, might bring up for each of them in relation to themselves, and their relationship? I knew now that if my husband and I had opened ourselves up to these experiences it would never have fixed our marriage. It may have prolonged it slightly, but I believe that, for me, it would have brought up a whole host of new insecurities and anxieties. It was hard enough to be in a couple, especially when I couldn't love who I was—when I didn't even *know* who I was.

I had a text from her the next morning: *We had a lovely time meeting you and enjoyed our time together. I was tired at the end and possibly didn't communicate that very well. It was nothing you did; I was just ready to go home.*

My journal shows that October was horrific for me.

I am not doing awfully well, but I am trying very, very hard.

It marked a regression in a lot of ways. Things with the Rower had ended abruptly and with no closure whatsoever. I lost my appetite again and as a result lost even more weight. I began vomiting again. I started drinking heavily and stopped making healthy choices. Insomnia returned with a vengeance. I was in an immense amount of physical pain. It felt as though I hadn't made any progress. As though I had just wasted the last six months fawning over these strangers—and for what?

Amelia came to visit me in Commodore Street, and we lazed the day away on my rooftop. Her departure for a work dinner later that day left a rather tipsy Charlotte alone with her thoughts, which was always a dangerous time for any unwitting contacts in my phone, and anyone I happened to be speaking to on the apps. I could feel myself spiralling and decided to sober up with a walk around Sydney Park. As I entered the park, I walked past a man who smelled of my husband's aftershave and for a brief moment I wanted to absorb him, to take that feeling of familiarity and swallow it whole.

Blasting The Smiths' 'Heaven Knows I'm Miserable Now' through my AirPods, I rounded a corner and, as I began to march up a hill, I locked eyes with my husband. Shocked, still tipsy and without one iota of coordination, I turned and ran straight for the bushes, fell dramatically, grazed my knee and hid, praying for the sake of my last remaining shred of dignity that he wasn't about to walk down that hill and therefore straight into me. I waited in the bushes for several minutes then sheepishly emerged, my woollen jumper now covered in sticks and leaves, and scurried home.

I felt red raw, exposed. Seeing my husband had brought home to me just how far I was from where I wanted to be, where I thought I should be. I needed to take a step back, delete the apps and stop looking to other people to provide the love and sense of worth I wasn't yet able to give myself. But first, I had to hit rock bottom . . .

The Fright and I met on Bumble and I was immediately drawn to his openness and his willingness to be vulnerable.

> I'm an open book. I can actually be too transparent at
> times. But it's part of me that likes to cast a wide net and
> say, 'Hey, look at me and everything I'm about,' and the
> people who are still with me after that are ones I know I
> can connect with deeply.

He was thirty-two, a social worker who specialised in mental health management—at least that was what he told me—and I remember gushing to a friend about how mature and articulate he seemed. We met in Newtown and walked to my favourite local haunt, Bloodwood. He was a bit reserved, but charming, wearing black jeans with an unbuttoned flannel shirt over a tee.

While I was so enjoying the depth and detail of our meandering conversation, I realised quite quickly that I hadn't finished two sips of my wine before he was already ordering another one. *Nerves*, I thought.

Two hours in, and his drinking hadn't slowed. I can't explain why—an instinct maybe—but I suddenly decided I should head home, alone. I didn't want to get drunk and I certainly didn't want to sleep with him, so I wrapped things up, saying that I would like to see him again but that I had made plans to meet a friend for dinner.

FADE

As I left and began the short walk home along King Street, I received a text from him saying, *I love you.* And then another. And another.

Rattled, I flagged down a taxi and climbed in—shaking, sweating, nauseous. I hurriedly explained the situation to the driver and asked him to drive me home the long way, to prevent any possibility that the Fright might follow.

Once home, I turned on every light, shut every curtain. I checked the doors were locked. Then I checked again.

What followed was a sleepless night filled with a flurry of text messages and a barrage of calls from the Fright. A night of harassment. Of anger and abuse. Of suicide threats.

I can't fucking believe this has happened.

I wish I was dead.

Please don't give up on me.

I really thought I had found something.

You were meant to bring balance to the force, not destroy it!

I'll fucking kill myself.

With shaking hands I messaged back:

I didn't know what to do, who to ask for help or what to say. I suppose now, many may wonder why I had not simply blocked him and upon reflection, I have wondered this myself. But I knew he was not okay; I knew what was happening was not right and having grown up in an environment with someone with mental health challenges it is now impossible for me not to be empathetic. It is impossible for me not to want to help when I see someone struggling, whether I know them or not. So I sent him the number for Lifeline and told him there were people he could talk to, people other than me.

But the texts kept coming, thick and fast. I felt like I couldn't breathe. I was too afraid to shower. I couldn't watch TV or turn on music. I couldn't concentrate. Couldn't eat. I set up camp in the front room where I could listen for the gate and I saved my neighbours' numbers, triple zero and Newtown police to the favourites list in my iPhone. I drafted SOS text messages in the notes app so that I could quickly copy and paste them if I needed them. I immediately went on Bumble and not only blocked but reported him.

His texts were relentless.

FADE

I hate you.

I'm going to jump off a bridge.

I fucking fell for you and now what the fuck.

By 2 am, I couldn't take it anymore. Every new message alert had me verging on the brink of full-blown hysteria. I wrote:

Please leave me alone.

He responded immediately.

No.

At 4.55 am he sent me a link to a YouTube video of Jackie Wilson's 'To Be Loved'. At 9.29 am he sent another flurry of messages, beginning with an apology.

Thanks so much for looking out for me. It was so great to meet you. I wish you all the best. Truly.

You're amazing and I want the best for you.

I just wanted so much to be good that I was so bad. I ruined it. I get it. I'd love you forever.

I'd give anything that I was something. I. Get. It.

> I fucking tried.
>
> Wow.

I didn't respond to any of them.

There was a pause of some hours and then, at 2.38 pm, the messages began again.

> Don't go. Please.
>
> I'm in hospital.
>
> I can't believe this. As soon as I get discharged I'm killing myself. Nice to know you.
>
> I'm a nice man who deserves a nice woman and as long as I don't touch drugs or alcohol I'm fine. I don't want to lose you.
>
> You don't like the drunk version of me—neither do I—and you never need meet him again. But the healthy part of me can give you so, so much more. I really like you, Charlotte.

He seemed calmer now, more rational, so I stupidly engaged:

> I really need to look after myself at the moment and that means wishing you all the best, and going our separate ways.

He wrote back:

> I understand. There's no justifying my actions. Nothing
> was ever said to you that was mean when I was sober.
> I'm not toxic. I'm not co-dependent. I have goals. I know
> who and what I want to be. I like who I am. And I like you.
> And I want to look out for you, look after you, and make
> you happy. All I need is another chance.

Feeling I'd made myself clear, I didn't acknowledge this, and
so the hounding began again.

> I'm sorry.
>
> I promise that I would never drink around you again.
>
> I wish I could just explain what happens to me when I
> drink too much.
>
> Please just don't give up.
>
> I see this is pointless. I know what I did was scary and
> unattractive. It's literally just what happens when I get
> too wasted. I was nervous. I didn't know how to act.
> I liked you and it frightened me. And I could tell that you
> liked me too. I just need a chance to make things okay.
> I have so much to give. I won't message you again. I'm
> sorry this happened. All I know is how much I would love
> to make it up to you.

I wrote:

> I found your actions and following messages incredibly
> troubling and upsetting. I really think it's best for you
> to look after yourself. This year has been incredibly
> challenging for me and I left a toxic long-term
> relationship only to experience more toxicity since.
> I can't put myself in that position again. I hope you
> understand. Goodbye and take care.

There were no more messages after this, and that night I slept deeply. The next morning, I woke up at 7 am to another message—not from the Fright this time, but from a woman who identified herself as his sister.

> Hi Charlotte, it's Natalie. I'm not sure how close you
> guys were but I feel it's right to tell you that he died from
> an overdose last night. I'm sorry if you two were close.
> Call me if you need to talk as I have his phone and I'm
> messaging his friends.

I couldn't stop shaking. I was horrified. I was traumatised. But then it dawned on me. If his sister was going through the Fright's messages, she would have seen her brother had sent me a barrage of abuse. Who could possibly interpret that as close? It wasn't his sister at all, I suspected; the Fright himself had sent the message. This was just a game to him, and I was the pawn. He was attention-seeking in the most manipulative way. I knew I needed a strategy. I had to break the third wall.

I found his Facebook profile, and from this I found his mother's and sister's profiles. It was a risk, but I sent a message to his sister, with a screenshot of the last text message. I expressed my condolences and explained that he and I were not close, that I had only met him once and I wished her well.

My friend Chris came over for a dinner that tasted only of the effort it took to make. He could see the bags under my eyes, that I was unsteady on my feet. I explained what had happened. He decided to call the Fright on a blocked number to see who answered.

After three rings, we heard his voice on the other end of the line: 'Hello?'

Clearly, he was very much alive. I deleted the message I'd sent to his sister, for fear that it would only make the harassment begin again. I messaged his profile picture to my girlfriends who were on the dating apps, telling them to watch out and to report him if they heard from him. Bumble finally responded to my report to say they had deleted his profile. It didn't stop him from creating another and another.

Two days later he sent me a link on YouTube to Black Sabbath's 'Changes'.

My anxiety was through the roof. I became afraid to leave the house. Fearful that, as we'd met at a bar only a ten-minute walk away, he was going to be somewhere close by. Watching out for me. Waiting.

Rob picked me up and, in an attempt to lift me out of my spiralling anxiety, took me on the ferry to Cremorne. We spent the afternoon swimming at Maccallum Pool. Rob had brought sandwiches made with slices of thickly buttered fresh white bread and beautifully glazed ham carved from the bone, but I couldn't eat. We decided to walk to Mosman Bay wharf and take the ferry home from there. As we were walking, I received another text from the Fright.

Please just love me.

I broke down. And I did what has always been the hardest thing for me to do—I asked for help.

Rob took my hand and led me to the back deck of Mosman Rowers. He fetched me a glass of water and then, together, we composed a message.

You MUST understand that, drunk or sober, your words carry an immense amount of weight. Pretending to have committed suicide is a horrific thing for anyone to do, let alone someone who claims to work in mental health. I find your actions abhorrent, unacceptable and absolutely terrifying.

I won't indulge this behaviour any longer. I do not know you. I do not owe you anything.

I do not want to hear from or see you again.

He responded immediately.

This is the saddest text I have ever received in my life.

Rob and I waited for the ferry back to Circular Quay, trying to figure out my next step. I could call the police, but I didn't know where he lived. I didn't have more than his name, phone number and one picture. There was his Facebook profile, of course, but it offered very little additional information. Because I had blocked and reported him on Bumble, I could no longer view his profile to source more photographs. We realised that, until now, the Fright and I had been alone in this twisted mindfuck. Perhaps the intervention of a third party, a male, would compel him to stop. So Rob sent him a message directly, from his own phone.

Charlotte's friend here. She's brought me completely up to date with your harassment. I know she has asked repeatedly for you to stop contacting her. Please stop, or we'll have to consider further measures.

The Fright's response was swift:

The Fright: Cool, man—by which I mean I'll stop. Please just let her know how sorry I am. I just don't know why I do this shit.

> *Rob*: I highly recommend you seek help,
> because you can't expect strangers to carry you.
> Not Charlotte, not me.

The Fright: Fuck you, dipshit. I don't expect anyone to carry me. Me and Charlotte had a wonderful time together.

> *Rob*: I'm in no place to deal with this, and more than
> happy to report your behaviour to the police. It's
> unacceptable. And don't even think about contacting
> Charlotte—your actions have caused so much
> damage to one of the closest people in my life.

The Fright: All right. I'll stop. And I deleted Charlotte's number. No police, yeah?

> *Rob*: I know it is hard from the privileged position
> us men have in society, but this kind of behaviour—
> pursuing contact when someone explicitly asked

FADE

you to stop contacting them—is called stalking. And
I assume from your studies in mental health and
counselling, you would know the fear and anxiety this
instils in women, when one woman dies every week in
Australia at the hands of a man.

Time passed, and then I had one final message.

Not a day has gone by since acting so poorly that your
voice has not entered my head at some point saying,
'I find your actions abhorrent.' I self-sabotage the
good things I have in my life, because my self-worth is
so low, that I feel I don't deserve anything, as well as
the feeling that I am going to inevitably mess things
up anyway. And threatening suicide when I'm in that
state is something that seems within the realm of being
reasonable. I couldn't be more self-loathing about
acting that way. This isn't a justification—for I know that
there isn't one, which makes it all the more frustrating.
Accepting accountability for my actions and realising
that self-will has consequences, is something I struggle
with greatly. You're a wonderful person. I'm glad you got
to see the real me for the few honest hours that I was just
me. Goodbye, Charlotte.

A memory from my childhood . . . My mum is sitting at the dining table with a friend having a conversation about mental illness and self-medicating. She's explaining how she doesn't smoke, drink or take drugs, that she doesn't self-medicate. Her friend is nodding, but when he speaks it is not to agree with her. 'You self-medicate,' he tells my mum. 'You eat too much. You self-medicate with food.'

Growing up and into my young adulthood, I never took drugs. I had no problem with drinking—passion pop, raspberry cruisers, vodka double blacks. But I never took drugs of any kind. I had a pathological fear of them. I thought that the drug would sense that I had mental illness in my genetics, and hurtle me into a drug-induced psychosis from which I could not return.

In the aftermath of my experience with the Fright, my brain was in a constant state of hypervigilance. I saw threats everywhere, my anxiety went into overdrive, and I turned to drinking to quiet a mind that just wouldn't give me a moment's peace. I drank. And I drank and I drank. And. I. Drank.

Drink. Vomit. Black out. Rinse. Repeat.

Drinking made me self-righteous. I would wake up to find on my phone the late-night (or early-morning) passive-aggressive drunk texts I had sent to my husband, who was either mature enough—or so bored by them and me—to simply ignore and forget. This only made me more bitter and resentful, more careless and reckless. I had no off switch.

My drinking was causing damage to the people around me—and to myself. I sensed that even my closest friends were beginning to tire of me. Their patience was wearing thin. So I did what any completely irrational person might do, and I began to sabotage my friendships. It was as though I wanted my friends to feel about me how I felt about myself. I wanted to make sure they understood what I knew to be true: that I was unlovable.

When I finally visited the Oracle, she told me she could feel the weight of me as soon as I entered the room. I confessed to her that I was worried about my mental health, that I felt *flat*, and she suggested that I try a six-month course of antidepressants, just as a circuit breaker. When I handed over the prescription, the pharmacist said dismissively that it probably wouldn't work. And my body must have noted this: I began to bruise terribly and had a severely upset stomach. I couldn't keep anything down and I hardly slept. I'd barely started taking the pills before I stopped.

I was increasingly fragile, vulnerable in ways I never had been before. I was stuck in a horrific cycle of self-loathing and would while away my days on social media, constantly checking my husband's dormant profiles for any updates on the life he was living without me. And I still hadn't deleted the dating apps. I knew I should. I knew I should take some time out to rest and recover. But I was convinced that the only thing that would make me feel better was to meet someone.

But then, a year after I had left my husband, my grandma died, and suddenly nothing else mattered.

After I heard the news, I sat on the floor and I howled. I was trying to process the immense heartache of losing the woman who wrote me letters each month on beautiful floral notepaper. The woman who welcomed me into her home every school holidays, when my father could not. She would pack picnic baskets full of egg sandwiches and take me to art galleries, or libraries, or churches. She took me to Europe when I was thirteen, and she showed me a world of beauty in a bowl of creamy white asparagus soup. Her shortbread recipe still brings me warmth and happiness whenever I bake it. She had an immense love of food, and she taught me that homemade food was best and that there was always time to pack a lunch before exploring the world. I still miss her audible sounds of enjoyment when she ate something she loved.

Grandma's funeral was held in an open-air cathedral near Forster. Her coffin was made from wicker, just like the picnic baskets she used to carry on our day trips. On top of the coffin, instead of flowers, were vegetables: carrots, cauliflower, radishes, brussels sprouts, tomatoes and capsicum. It suited my grandma perfectly. When we returned to our family holiday home, the emotion of the day had begun to take its toll. I was starving. As I entered, the smell of something delicious wafted past me. I found my extended family eating soup by the bowlful—my aunty had repurposed the vegetable arrangement into a heartwarming dinner for us all. This was so Grandma, and *so* Ree.

After the funeral, I took the train back to Sydney. The immediate shock of grief had passed, but my head ached. The rhythmic sway of the train soothed me. And I slept.

In our final session with the Guide, which took place in our separate households over Zoom, she told my ex-husband and me that she felt as though we were 'growing up'. That when we grow up, we finally discover who we are within. When we grow up with somebody, we get to the point of questioning whether we are thinking and acting in a certain way because that is how we want to, and need to, or if that's how our partner would want us to and need us to. Wanting something more for yourself, wanting to expand your needs, she explained, is your right, and it is what will ultimately make you feel fulfilled.

Somewhere along the way, my ex-husband and I stopped thinking of each other and began to think only of ourselves. More and more, now, I think he and I actually came to the decision to end our marriage together. Rather than me deciding to leave, it was a case of us putting ourselves first. Together. Despite all the hurt and pain, we had loved each other, but we'd had the courage to let go, to love ourselves more.

I began thinking about the last few months of self-sabotage. I wanted to let the chaos of them fall away. I wanted to shed my skin. My body was telling me that I needed to nurture myself. I was determined to be okay on my own.

But then my divorce papers were delivered.

Regret. I will never say the word when it comes to my marriage. That isn't to say I don't live with regrets. Of course I do. I regret all those times I said 'yes' when I really wanted to say 'no'. I regret putting so much emphasis on what people thought of me, rather than what *I* thought of me. I regret taking life, and myself, too seriously. I regret letting my relationship with my absent father impact so many of my other relationships. I regret putting other people's needs, and happiness, before my own. But I do not regret marrying my husband. I did love him. I just wish I could have loved myself more.

I tore open the envelope and read the enclosed document. I read it again, over and over. I was crying and laughing, laughing and crying. I said out loud to no one in particular, 'Hello, I'm Charlotte Ree. I am thirty years old and I'm a divorcee.'

I felt a great sense of loss. Though not for my ex-husband, but for the family we had created together. For his mama and his aunty, Tia.

I loved them both, especially his mama, so very deeply. She had grace and style and we would always do the things that I never could with my mama—like facials, manicures and pedicures. When I first met my ex-husband, she was running her own restaurant and she taught me all about Italian food. She was the first person to show me how to use a pasta roller and how to make passata.

Sometimes the loss of her still makes me weep.

Easter fell that weekend, and I began to feel like I was being swept away by a landslide. I was so desperately alone. Rob was out of town, Ali was working in New York and Amelia was visiting her family. My own family were far away on the Mid North Coast. Even my traditional Easter treat—a box of Pasticceria Papa's chocolate hot-cross buns—weren't enough to comfort me. My emotional turmoil became physical, but rather than vomiting, as I usually did at such times, I began to experience chest pain. The pain ran up my left arm and behind my left breast, where a constant ache developed. I left it for a day or two, restless, but by the third it had become so painful I couldn't sleep. My breathing felt laboured, and my chest felt tight and heavy, like someone was sitting on it.

On Easter Sunday I took myself to the emergency room of St Vincent's Hospital. I explained that it felt as though my heart was beating out of my chest and I was seen by a nurse immediately. Initial tests showed that there were heart murmurs on my ECG.

I returned to the waiting room, where I was asked to fill in a patient information form with my medical history and contact details. It was the first time I'd been confronted with the question of my marital status, the first time I had to put a cross in the box beside 'divorced'. It was the first time since I was a child that, instead of listing my ex-husband as my next of kin, I had to list my mum.

A pain hit me in the chest with such immense force that I almost doubled over.

I handed the form back to the nurse, and a young doctor with kind eyes talked me through the next steps, explaining that they would take blood tests to measure my troponin levels. That they would need to do a chest X-ray to look at my heart. She warned me that I mustn't eat or drink anything, in case I needed to have surgery.

It was eight hours before all the results came in, and it turned out that there was nothing abnormal going on with my heart. The doctor took the time to sit with me, to ask me if there was anything happening in my life that could be causing me added stress and anxiety. As I explained my situation, it dawned on me what had happened: I had been suffering from a severe panic attack. It was only then that I realised just how connected my head and heart actually were.

As Bessel van der Kolk writes in his revolutionary book *The Body Keeps the Score*, 'bodies are constantly bombarded by visceral warning signs, and, in an attempt to control these processes, they often become expert at ignoring their gut feelings and in numbing awareness of what is played out inside. They learn to hide from their selves.' In entering a hyper-anxious state and having a panic attack, I had felt like I was knocked out of my body. Disassociating was my body's way of protecting itself when it is overwhelmed by its environment. The Oracle tells me it is a primal coping technique; we disassociate to conserve energy. Like a baby crying when it hasn't been fed. After a while, the baby stops crying. It shuts down. It conserves energy. It is a safety response, and we all do it. Now I needed to work hard to feel safe, to be myself. Even after all my therapy, I still found it so incredibly difficult to recognise when I was not in my own body. And to be me, the *real* me, I needed to find a way to be in my body *all* the time. So when I was spiralling out of control, when I felt overwhelmed by panic, I needed to go back to my body—to how I *felt*.

In my next session with the Oracle I learned that I had to take the time to calm my body. To pay attention to the parts that weren't comfortable, and try to understand what was making them feel that way. I needed to do my best to relax.

'It's like making pavlova,' the Oracle explained. 'You can't whip the egg whites into peaks until the bowl is clean and the eggs are at room temperature. If you want to make peaks, your body has to be as calm as possible. You need to slow down.'

And that's why my heart sang in moments spent with friends like Nadine, who surprised me with a box and a note. The note said: *A rosette for healing.* Inside the box was the most perfect handmade rosette with a deep navy ribbon and an illustration of a naked woman on the front. Beside her was a poem, 'always evolving', from Rupi Kaur's collection, *Home Body.* It was encouraging me to slow down, to sit with this version of myself. To just be, be in the moment.

feast

You don't have to belong to the drearily narcissistic learn-to-love yourself school of thought to grasp that it might be a good thing to consider yourself worth cooking for.

NIGELLA LAWSON, *HOW TO EAT*

How easy it can be to feel alone when we are fighting internal battles our friends know nothing about, or when living with a partner who doesn't see us.

If the first lockdown was a catalyst for my self-destruction, Sydney's second lockdown was a time of rebirth. It was winter, and after my one-year lease of the Newtown terrace ended I moved into a new apartment in Rushcutters Bay. The lockdown restrictions meant a forced hiatus from dating, and from hosting and cooking for friends, or friends of friends. I could no longer hide myself, or my pain, in cooking for others. I decided to delete all my profiles and remove the dating apps from my iPhone. That second lockdown, there was just me, and me alone.

I decided it was high time I showed myself the same level of care I'd been giving to others. I would be selfish with my energy, with my time. I would read books I hadn't read and reread ones I had. I would take an hour-long bath every day. I would FaceTime my beautiful grampy. I would go for long, solitary walks until I could feel my body tiring and my mind finally becoming still. And I would cook—not to nourish and bring pleasure to others, but to nurture myself. Because I was worthy of that care. Because I deserved it.

There is a Japanese word, *kuchisabishii*, that means 'lonely mouth' or 'longing to have or put something in one's mouth'. It's eating just to satisfy a craving. In lockdown, I had a lonely mouth. I think I'd spent so long feeding and nourishing others I forgot it was safe for me to swallow. To be in the moment, to soak it all in, to savour the pleasure against all the pain.

With my favourite restaurants closed and my itchy feet forced to remain stationary, I endeavoured to replicate at home some of the dishes I was craving most. Lockdown afforded me the luxury of time in which to do that. The time to spend a day making salty, sweet, starchy broths and stocks. To roll pasta dough and fill it and mould it into shape. I began to cook dishes that *took* me somewhere.

I spent close to forty-eight hours attempting to replicate a tortellini in brodo I had eaten in Bologna. I began with the broth itself—using the flesh and bones of chicken and pork and beef, as well as whole pieces of celery and carrot and onion—cooked slowly and then strained into a container and refrigerated overnight. I minced mortadella, prosciutto and pork loin for the filling, and rolled wafer-thin sheets of pasta, folding the filling into squares to make perfect little pockets. I made so many of them I was still rolling tortellini in my dreams that night.

I learned to make frittata by whisking three eggs with salt, pepper and parmesan and adding it to a frying pan of spinach that I had sautéed in olive oil. I then put it under the grill on high until it was golden and cooked through. I stuffed capsicums with halloumi and pork mince. I baked prawns with salty feta crumbled over the top and filled pockets of pita with it. I perfected cheese soufflé, which I watched rise through the oven door while sitting on my kitchen floor. I discovered the subtle art of a potato tortilla, and the comfort of a pea and ham hock soup. I jazzed up Japanese curries with the addition of soft egg omelettes and crispy chicken karaage. I learned to make rich and creamy tonkatsu broth and then paired it with homemade ramen noodles. In celebration of my independence, I cooked myself a gourmet tomahawk steak, because a steak bathed in pepper sauce is spectacularly satisfying. I fried the most sublime butter-basted piece of barramundi, with skin so crispy it snapped as I bit into it. For a snack, I coated lamb cutlets in panko crumbs and sea salt, or I steamed a medley of green vegetables and ate them with my fingers. I made rolled pork roasts with crackling—mostly so I could have leftovers for roast meat sandwiches—and all the trimmings. There was roast pumpkin and crispy potatoes, which of course I cooked in duck fat with rosemary and sea salt. And naturally, there were obscene amounts of gravy.

One of my most intense cravings during this time was wonton noodle soup. Specifically, the prawn wonton noodle soup found at Tsim Chai Kee Noodle Shop on Wellington Street in Hong Kong—not exactly something I could order in. Now, I am not saying that my wonton noodle soup rivals the one I found there, but I *am* saying that my recipe was the perfect antidote to my frustration at being unable to travel, as a single whiff of its broth was the equivalent to walking down Wellington Street, salivating in anticipation.

But what I really longed for, more than anything, was the restorative broth I had found in Udon Shin's udon noodle soup in Tokyo. This soup was beautifully simple and, like most things I cooked, a form of comfort—particularly when slurped on a cold winter's night. The recipe begins with instructions for making your own dashi stock, but you can use store-bought dashi stock powder if you are in a rush. I often made a big batch of it and froze it in solo lady portions.

Admittedly, I never had the patience required to make my own udon noodles, and always struggled to find a super-market offering worth my while—that is, until I discovered Kama-age Udon in the freezer of my local Asian supermarket. Made in Japan, they are snap-frozen and are the closest I have come to reliving my Udon Shin experience at home.

So much of my time in the kitchen was centred around the discovery that I was at my most productive and creative during periods of solitude. As Rilke wrote in *Letters to a Young Poet*, 'Your solitude will be a support and a home for you, even in the midst of very unfamiliar circumstances, and from it you will find all your paths.' Solitude. It's the joy of giving yourself permission to date yourself. Of discovering that you are, in fact, the best date that you can ever take out—or, better yet, cook for.

During lockdown, I shopped often—once every two or three days—and I was deliberate about it, only purchasing the things I would consume. Week after week I found myself placing the same items in my shopping basket: a loaf of uncut Sonoma miche to indulge my love of delicious grilled cheese sandwiches; a dozen free-range eggs, which I hard-boiled, covered in sea salt flakes and anointed in olive oil for the perfect snack; a capsicum—always red—which I would salt and cover in olive oil then chargrill to serve alongside guacamole, a crisp hash brown and a fried egg for a Mexican breakfast wrap; and, finally, fresh basil leaves and pine nuts so I could whip up Pa's pesto when I needed my fix of home.

But there were also moments when I wanted to treat myself and divert from my staple shopping list, shunning my trusty freezer stash to make a three-course feast for one, poring over my many cookbooks and challenging myself to cook something luxurious and labour-intensive to enjoy all on my own. Because I knew now that I was worthy of my own love, care and cooking. That I should take the time and effort to feed myself.

Slowly, by starting simply and rediscovering my joy for these nostalgic meals, I began to crave more. I began to find a sense of *play* in cooking. A sense of stillness. Of presence. Of *joy*. I was returning to what had initially made me fall in love with baking but without the attendant anxiety, without the desperate acts of service that cooking had morphed into. I became more confident. I was finding more pleasure in the process of cooking and devouring delicious self-sustaining dishes than I had in one-night stands. I was beginning to *like* myself again.

As restrictions eased and Sydney began to open up, I realised that I loved to take myself out for dinner. I would spend hours researching the restaurants I wanted to eat at and the food I wanted to order, and often arrived without a booking to find a spare seat at the bar or a tiny single table hidden in the back corner of the restaurant, surrounded by couples or groups of family and friends.

Initially, I was intimidated by the idea of eating alone, self-conscious about my solitary state, but I soon got over it. I discovered that, like cooking, dining alone is an activity in which I find myself being completely present. I would put away my phone and either read a book or, better still, watch the people around me and sometimes engage in conversation with the people seated beside me, or the amazing staff who served me.

There were two restaurants in my neighbourhood that I began to frequent. The first was Gaku Robata Grill, my favourite Japanese restaurant in Sydney, where I would turn up just after opening time to be given a rare single seat at the bar. Robata refers to the method of slow-grilling ingredients over a flat grill that sits above hard-wood charcoal and, as their menu states, the results are 'dramatic and delicious'. I ordered salted edamame, agedashi tofu with zucchini flower tempura, yaki onigiri served with sweet soy sauce and whipped A5 Wagyu fat, and the best aburi salmon nigiri I've eaten outside of Japan. The chef handed each morsel to me directly, and as I sipped yuzu sake served over ice, I found myself immediately transported back to the sushi bar I'd discovered in the depths of an Osaka train station, where I'd eaten three nights in a row.

Then there was my beloved Bar Vincent. I had been there so often and developed such a close friendship with the owners, Sarah and Andy, that I was able to order half and three-quarter portions of pasta dishes—the perfect solution for a solo diner whose eyes are far bigger than her stomach. I drank lambrusco and ate crumbed scallops, copious amounts of their house-made bread with salted butter, handmade capellini with pipis and tortellini in a creamy bechamel sauce with freshly grated nutmeg. One night, as my tortellini arrived, and a generous glass of light Italian red was poured, I began to speak to my neighbours at the bar, who ended up giving me a tarot card reading. It was wonderfully unexpected, as nights like those can be when you open yourself up to the unknown.

I learned that allowing yourself to be cooked *for* and to be *served* was as important, if not more important, as doing it for others.

I savoured the final moments of lockdown, and I was reminded of small pleasures I had sorely missed. The joy of smiling at someone without a mask, using the movement of our mouths to say what our eyes can't always communicate. Physical touch. Side-splitting laughter with friends and seeing and cooking for them. Being carefree. Spontaneity. Spontaneity. Spontaneity. Overwhelmingly, I felt immense gratitude. Gratitude for what I saw as this gift of time. Gratitude for the continued deep dive of self-discovery. But I also felt torn. Torn between the beautiful nurturing bubble of solitude I had created, and the social butterfly that was ready to burst from within. I couldn't wait to see people in the flesh after so many months of Zoom and FaceTime and text messages. To finally hug my friends and family, hold them close and tight in a big, beautiful embrace.

I am overwhelmingly grateful for those few months of solitude. They were *hard.* For some, the forced shutdown caused the collapse of marriages, the reassessment of lives, the Great Resignation, the beginning of new careers and businesses, financial hardship, and even unanticipated pleasures.

As for me, the lockdown helped me to rediscover myself. To fall in love not with someone else, but with myself.

Just as the first lockdown helped me to discover the joy of cooking for others, the joy of serving and feeding and sustaining and giving and providing, the second time around I learned there is also an immense joy to be found in cooking an extravagant meal all on your own. A meal that no one else will see. That no one else will taste. That no one else will judge. Its sole purpose is to nourish and sustain just one person—you.

full

Anyway, whatever it is, don't be afraid of its plenty.
Joy is not made to be a crumb.

MARY OLIVER, 'DON'T HESITATE'

For a long time, I was plagued by self-awareness. Obsessed with outcomes, paralysed by fear of judgement. I couldn't just *be*. I rarely, if ever, found myself being present in the moment. I was so obsessed with being in control that I never wanted to step out of my comfort zone. I was afraid. Afraid of new experiences.

When my divorce was finalised and our second lockdown began, I peeled each layer of myself back, like an onion, to become my most raw and vulnerable. The hard part was not the act of peeling the layers away, but acknowledging them, making the conscious and deliberate decision to say *yes*. To say yes to love. Yes to joy. Yes to new experiences and yes to changing my perspective on my old ones. To try almost everything, at least once, and see what stuck.

I wrote this mantra in my journal and I repeated it to myself at my lowest ebb—now I recite it when I'm at my happiest, too, as it still holds so much weight.

> *Have the **courage** to be imperfect*
>
> *Have the **compassion** to show kindness to yourself, and to others*
>
> *Have **connection** as a result of authenticity.*

People always say that you will meet someone when you least expect it. Timing is everything. The work I had done to come to understand and accept myself allowed me to embark on the beginning of a love story—both with myself and with the man I came to call the Ginger.

After spending valuable time rediscovering who I was, and undergoing some significant changes, it was time to turn my focus outwards again. I rejoined the dating apps, and at the end of June 2021 I matched with the Ginger on

Tinder. He was a wedding photographer and, more than that, I discovered, he was a storyteller. I noticed straight away that there was something different about him from the other men I had engaged with online previously. Perhaps it was his way with words; he articulated himself beautifully and succinctly. There was also his reciprocal openness and honesty about the aftermath of the break-up of his previous long-term relationship. When I shared with him the turmoil and anxiety I had experienced in the wake of my divorce, he sent me a link to a post he had written after his own break-up, in which he wrote that his 'anxiety at times was (and is) crippling', and that he struggled to face the prospect of narrating other people's love stories while his own was crumbling around him. I think what struck me the most about this post, and the others I read, was his insight and self-awareness. We exchanged numbers and, given Sydney was still in lockdown, planned a walk for the following Sunday.

As our walking date approached, I suggested he come over for dinner, telling him that he could pick the music and I would cook for him. He told me he was a vegetarian and wrote:

Ballsy of you to invite a strange man from the internet to your house for dinner. I mean, I'm delightful, but you can't really know that yet.

Before he arrived, he sent me a link to the playlist he'd made, which gave me an immediate insight into him and his brilliant sense of humour. The title, 'Truth, Beauty and a Picture of Dan-And-you-s', picked up on a throwaway comment I'd made on the crush I'd developed on Victorian premier Dan Andrews thanks to his daily press conferences. It was full of music by The Temptations, Paul Simon, William Bell, Gang of Youths, Dusty Springfield and The Whitlams—and, of course, it included the now infamous 'Get on the Beers', Mashd N Kutcher's remix of a press conference in which the premier exhorted Victorians to do just that.

After living so long for just one person, me, I became nervous at the thought of dating again, so I decided to make Pa's pesto, which never failed to calm me. I mixed it with fresh ricotta and a sprinkling of sea salt flakes and placed tablespoonfuls between wafer-thin sheets of handmade pasta, which I had painstakingly rolled piece by piece. I then cut ravioli by hand using the ribbed brass pastry cutter I had purchased in Bologna many moons ago.

When the Ginger rang the doorbell, I buzzed him into my apartment building and then opened the front door. I had to tilt my head back to look up at the beautiful but hairy giant of a man, with his sun-bleached, curly blond hair and sun-kissed beard with tinges of ginger. He was wearing tight, black, well-worn skinny jeans, a cream button-up collared shirt and a faux fur–lined denim jacket. He was carrying two bottles of wine, which impressed me, because very few of my previous dates had ever thought to bring one bottle of wine, let alone two. His voice was deep, booming, and his laugh even louder. He filled up every corner of my apartment.

As we drank wine and chatted, I sautéed the now cooked, tender, translucent ravioli pillows I had made earlier in the day in a sauce of crispy sage and brown butter. But while I had made what I thought would be enough for two, I quickly realised I had served him the kind of portion I ate myself, which was certainly not enough for this friendly giant. He finished his bowl and then finished what was left of mine, but I'm sure he must still have been starving.

The conversation was stimulating, scintillating, but when it came to physical closeness, I was guarded. Protective of myself. He inched his chair closer and I scooted mine back. He leaned forward, and I leaned away. It wasn't until after we'd finished dinner and cleared the table that I finally relaxed into our date. When the first bottle of wine was drunk and the second nearly finished, we moved to the couch and I announced, 'I am going to kiss you now.'

Our kiss was all-consuming and we retreated to my bedroom. The night was a sleepless one for me for no other reason than I lay awake counting his breaths. They were few and far between. I later discovered he had sleep apnoea.

A few days after our first date I messaged him, asking if he wanted to come over for dinner the following night. He didn't reply for a few hours and, when he did, it was to say that, for reasons he couldn't quite put his finger on, he didn't think we'd work out in the long run, so him coming over might not be such a good idea. He said that he wasn't at all meaning to imply that he thought I was 'super into' him or 'wanting anything more than a bit of fun', but that he wanted to be completely transparent about how he was feeling.

I responded light-heartedly, saying that there was no need to overthink it.

His reply to this was confusing: 'I am not blowing smoke up your butt when I say I'm legit a bit sad we probably won't hang out again.'

I told him that the smoke screen was only coming from his end, and that I was around if he felt like catching up. He suggested that maybe he could cook for me 'and bring it over, as daunting as that would be'. He told me I had inspired him, that he had already spent about three hours in the kitchen that day.

On our second date, he made me an Ottolenghi chickpea soup with a rather bizarre addition of fresh pasta and sour cream which I still haven't quite reconciled myself to. It didn't matter what he had made, really; it was the fact that he'd gone to the trouble to cook for me that mattered.

After dinner, we once again retreated to the couch, and I asked him outright why he had been inclined to dismiss the possibility of another date at first.

Looking around my Art Deco apartment, he told me that I was the first woman he'd dated whose home was decorated with nice furniture and original art, and he'd made some assumptions about me on this basis—that I was a trust fund baby, perhaps, or a lady of leisure, or, as he so charmingly put it, a 'bougie asshole'.

I was taken aback. I knew that I tended to present myself in a certain way; to put up a protective wall and try to perform a version of myself that represented how I wanted to be seen. But it wasn't how I *needed* to be seen. So, I told him everything. I gave it all away, for nothing—with no expectations, only honesty. I told him about my quirky mama's bipolar disorder and the effect that her manic episodes had had on me, and still continued to have at times. I told him about the breakdown of my marriage. About the control I craved and the financial control my ex-husband exercised over me. I didn't shy away from the ugly parts of myself, either. I described my behaviour in my relationship and in my friendships, and how I longed to be liked and to be needed.

I told him everything because, for me, the only way to move forward was to be honest and vulnerable, raw and real, even if it meant baring my soul to someone I might only know fleetingly. Being honest like this was anxiety-inducing, though, especially when it meant revealing parts of myself that I didn't particularly like or even necessarily understand.

Very few people will explore *you* with you. I was on a quest to find someone who would like me not despite my imperfections and vulnerability, but *because* of them. And so the Ginger's text the following day made my heart sing.

> The fact you're clearly in such a great place mentally after what I can only imagine has been a tough couple of years on your own, as well as dealing with everything else you've been through, is legitimately really fucking inspiring. I can't say I'm proud of you because that sounds weird and disingenuous, and implies a knowledge of you back when you weren't this way, but I am legitimately really freaking happy for you. It would

have taken a lot of mental strength and fortitude and will to get there and implies a whole bunch of really great things about you. Even the fact you can open up about it to someone completely new is a testament to a lot of things, and alone says a lot about how much work you've done. It also made me realise I jumped to a lot of conclusions, probably unfairly, for which I'm sorry.

After we had been seeing each other for a few weeks, the Ginger invited me over to his house for dinner, but he warned me that he and his housemates would be having a few drinks and then skinny-dipping to celebrate finally being able to swim at Bronte. I reminded him that I grew up in the Northern Rivers and that a few nips and dicks wouldn't scare me. It was also just part of me opening myself up again, stepping out of my comfort zone and trying something new.

To my surprise and delight, I was made to feel welcome in his home immediately, and from the beginning I was at ease. His housemates had a huge part to play in that, too—Ken and Kirsty felt like old friends, like people I had always known.

For dinner, the Ginger made us warm bowls of laksa topped with lemongrass tofu. For our post-swim dessert, I made a chocolate twist on the olive oil cake from *Just Desserts*, which, to cater for Kirsty's dietary requirements, was free of both gluten and dairy. It was so moist and so delicious when we returned shivering from our midnight winter swim, we couldn't stop at one slice.

What followed were many shared meals, but unlike with the men I'd dated previously, the effort put into our dates was mutual. The Ginger not only brought me home-cooked dinners but homemade cookie dough, too. When I did find myself cooking for our dates, I found him by my side. We cooked together.

After months of obsessively trawling through various rental listings, I finally discovered my dream apartment a few hundred metres away from my current place. Unlike my previous apartment, it was bathed in sunlight, being located on the top floor of four never-ending flights of stairs. The apartment itself was petite, just thirty-two metres square, but it had a private rooftop terrace bigger than the apartment itself that truly stole my heart. It was the third time I had moved in less than eighteen months, but it was the first time moving felt exciting rather than unsettling. I had unpacked and settled in within forty-eight hours of opening the front door, with all the furniture in place and artwork hung.

On my first Friday night in my new home, I was excited, because the Ginger was coming over. He would be the first person to visit.

I buzzed him into the building when he arrived, then waited by the front door, but it seemed to be taking him an inordinate amount of time to climb the stairs.

I realised he'd missed my text explaining how to get to the front door and had gone up the wrong set of stairs. When I opened my back door, I found him sweating profusely and short of breath. He was exhausted because he had been carrying something ridiculously heavy and awkward: a beautiful big apple cactus. He remembered that I had been missing the succulents I'd had on my rooftop in Commodore Street so he'd decided to propagate and bring me a piece of his own. I was overcome by his thoughtfulness.

He was also carrying a bottle of Taittinger, and he proceeded to teach this lifelong lover of bubbles a skill she had never known and cannot believe she had ever lived without— how to sabre a bottle of champagne.

Later that week, I sent the Ginger a piece of my writing. It was an essay I had written for the August issue of *Vogue* magazine. It is the first time I had written about my divorce. It was an essay on how my philosophy on life had shifted over the past year of cooking, eating and living for just me. Writing that piece gave me the courage to write this book, in fact; it was like a dress rehearsal.

I felt incredibly anxious after sending it to him, but he wrote later that same day to tell me that he found the essay to be 'brave and honest and introspective'.

The following week, he came over with his camera to take a photo of me that I could use to promote it. That was the first time I had ever been photographed by a lover. I felt shy and awkward, but he slowly brought me out of my shell by doing what he does when he is shooting photos of his couples at their weddings—by asking questions, by listening. At one point, as I stood in my new kitchen, bathed in the light of the tiny porthole window, he asked me if I could call to mind a moment after I had left my marriage that, if I looked back to it now, made me realise just how far I had come.

In an instant I was transported back to my kitchen in the house on Commodore Street, an untouched boiled egg sitting threateningly in front of me. I recalled how I'd had no appetite for a life that, at the time, felt devoid of colour and taste.

When he edited the photo and sent it to me later that morning, I struggled to look at it. There was no filter, no make-up, no enhancing or tweaking. Just me. It was as if I was seeing myself for the first time in my life. And not only that, I felt *seen* by someone else for the first time, too.

This was reinforced when I sent the photo to Grampy, who responded: 'I didn't feel like I'd really seen you until that photo. I feel as though I've finally got to know you.'

Sharing that essay, and the photograph that accompanied it, was as terrifying as it was liberating. It was the beginning of me presenting myself in public exactly how I was now in private: honest and vulnerable and accepting.

The responses were everything I could have hoped for and more, and the most impactful ones came from the most surprising of places. I received messages from peers in high school.

I know we haven't spoken in a while, but I wanted to acknowledge the strength it took to share your vulnerability with others, one wrote.

You've always been one of the strong ones. Even when I first met you as a fifteen-year-old, it's one of the first things I noticed about you, commented another.

Authors whom I had toured with wrote to me, too. *The article is brilliant for so many reasons . . . not least of all for its clear-eyed self-analysis and honesty. NO is definitely a powerful word—especially when it comes to self-care*, said one.

Even my ex-husband passed on his support and congratulations.

But it was the messages I received from people I didn't know, the ones from complete strangers, that gave me goosebumps.

Charlotte, you have inspired me to cook up a single ladies special dinner tonight just for solo me in lockdown. Thanks for the reminder to treat and care for myself!

It takes most of us years to realise we have to look after ourselves first.

Resonating so much with my own story and journey of grief, love of self and cooking.

Food is the ingredient that binds us all together.

They made me laugh, too. Like the man who, referring to my description of the many meals I had cooked for those many men, suggested: *Maybe rustle up some meat pies and hot chips and see how that works? And yes, I love mushy peas! The sure-fire way to a man's heart.*

The moment I read that comment, my doorbell buzzed. It was a courier: I had a delivery waiting for me downstairs.

I descended the four flights and was greeted by a brand-new polaroid camera, a custard tart—just like the ones Pa used to buy me from Crusty's Bakehouse in Lismore—and a hand-written note from the Ginger: *'Cause custard tarts and polaroids are back in Vogue.*

What struck me most about the Ginger was I was as excited by the ideas and goals and ambitions he had as I was by my own. We were encouraging one another's paths and creative endeavours. We were putting our hands up to support and uplift one another without hesitation or question. To be each other's sounding boards and cheerleaders. To celebrate each other's accomplishments as if they were our own. I had found in him someone with so much heart, so much belief in me, that I could no longer doubt I was capable of becoming exactly who I had always wanted to be. I believe it was a first for both of us, to have someone see us like that. To have someone who was beginning to feel like a partner, in every sense of the word. It occurred to me that a partner does not complete you; they inspire you to complete yourself. And that's why, as exciting as it was to be cared for, I also made time to take care of myself. I was careful not to neglect myself, not to lose myself in the excitement of developing our relationship.

I decided to make myself a fancy solo dinner to celebrate the publication of my article in *Vogue*. I made a playlist of sixties love songs and the filthiest martini of olive brine, dry vermouth and vodka (never gin). As I started to cook, I was serenaded by the voices of Ella, Marvin and Aretha, and my version of self-love and self-care began.

I started with a wedge of deliciously creamy French brie recommended by my cheesemonger, Penny, which I ate with a crusty French baguette. The beautiful rib-eye steak from my local butcher was salted and seared to perfection (we solo diners don't treat ourselves to steak nearly enough) and served with a creamy pepper sauce. The first bite was so tender and so buttery it made me question if my attempts to join the Ginger in being a virtuous vegetarian were futile. The accompanying leafy greens and vegetables had been sourced from the local Saturday morning market. Dessert was my favourite offering from Flour and Stone—Nadine's quince custard tart.

The Ginger had introduced me to his friends, and now it was my turn to introduce him to mine. I arranged to meet Rob and some other close friends at Blackwattle Bay for a picnic. I baked David Lovett's focaccia studded with cherry tomatoes and rosemary sprigs, and as we sat by the bay eating and drinking, and I watched my friends and my new lover get to know each other, the whole afternoon felt effortless. As comfortable as it all was, though, I couldn't help but feel scared. I recognised I was beginning to fall for this man.

When we later returned to my rooftop, having consumed a few too many bottles of wine, we pulled my bedspread and feather pillows out onto my terrace and lay together under the stars. I told the Ginger that I was beginning to develop feelings for him. That I didn't expect those feelings to be returned straight away, and that I certainly didn't expect him to reciprocate there and then, but in the spirit of honesty, transparency and self-preservation, if he didn't feel that this— us—was something he wanted to pursue, then we would need to go our separate ways.

We kissed tentatively, and then I went to fetch some more wine. When I returned, Frank Sinatra's 'My Way' was blasting through the speakers. I discovered the Ginger wrapped in the bedspread, balancing himself on the roof's ledge carelessly, singing at the top of his lungs and smiling from ear to ear.

The next time the Ginger came over, he wasn't himself, and I began readying myself for the beginning of the end. We sat on the terrace and, as the sun set, he started to cry as he said something so boyishly sweet: 'I feel like I've only dated girls before, and you're a woman.'

He told me he had feelings for me too, that he wanted to pursue this and see where it was going, no matter where we might end up.

The following morning, we ventured to North Bondi with his housemates. He made me a flask of English breakfast tea and I sat perched on the rocks, engrossed in the pages of my book as they donned their wetsuits to go for a dive. What I didn't know then was that a few short months later I would be wearing my own wetsuit, flippers and snorkel to jump in right alongside them. What I *did* know then was that I didn't have to do anything special to *make* the Ginger like me or want to spend time with me. I didn't need to buy anything, prove anything or take him anywhere. I just needed to be me. I realised I was happiest, most present, most myself when we were just hanging out, doing ordinary things. The important thing was, though my happiness was enhanced by him, it wasn't dependent on him.

After the ravioli of our first date I had stopped trying to impress him with elaborate meals, and it was three whole months before I next went all out and made a three-course feast for the Ginger. The meal began with zucchini flowers stuffed with stracciatella and mint that were then lightly battered and fried. For the main, I made what can best be described as a labour of love in the form of my eggplant parmigiana, and I followed this with tiramisu for dessert. The whole experience was eye-opening. I realised I was returning to an old version of myself, but this time with someone I actually liked. Someone whom I wanted to feed and nourish and care for, while at the same time nourishing and caring for myself.

There was a hunger in both of us in those first few months which was impossible to satisfy. Julia Child once said about her husband Paul, 'If we could just have the kitchen and the bedroom, that would be all we need.' And that was true of me and the Ginger. Sex, like the rest of our relationship, was a place of safety infused with play: a place where each of us could explore and communicate and develop a sense of understanding about ourselves for the first time, with the unconditional support of the other.

The Ginger kept telling me that he didn't know where this—where we—were going.

'I don't know if this will become something or will be a lockdown thing or what will happen, but I'm very grateful for it regardless.'

As Amelia reminded me, neither of us could know where this relationship would go.

That's the thing. You can't predict the future. But you can decide what you *want* the future to look like.

My favourite activity has always been to *eat*. Then to talk to anyone who will listen about all the delicious things that I have eaten. And *then*, most importantly, to think about what I want to eat *next*. But I have come to realise, when it's coming from a healthy place—and without the anxiety and turmoil that used to accompany it—my favourite activity is to *feed*. I swear I spent the majority of that second lockdown dreaming of dragging my dining table onto the rooftop terrace. I craved long lunches that would turn into late-night dinners and kitchen dance parties. It's what I looked forward to most as Sydney slowly started to open up again. Especially now that my desire to host was coming from a position of self-care rather than servitude. By inviting people into my home, I am really inviting them into my heart. I am inviting them to see and experience me at my most raw and real and relatable.

In October, I decided to host a dinner for my friends. I spent the entire day cooking in the galley kitchen of my tiny apartment, which had such limited counter space I found my preparations spilling over to the dining table. I started first thing in the morning with dessert. Perhaps I was subconsciously drawing on a joyful memory from my childhood, when Mama would serve my brother and me 'upside down dinners', with the sweet coming before the savoury. Really, though, desserts are what I look forward to the most, and by baking them first I know that my day and my dinner is always off to a delicious start.

Before I knew it, the day had disappeared, and just as I was ready to collapse into a chair with a glass of crisp white wine, the first guests arrived, and the sabring began.

For the first course, I had made my prawn wonton noodle soup in a broth that had been simmering slowly for eight hours. For the main, I used the drunken chicken from the broth to make a shredded chicken salad. I also made fried rice, mapo tofu and fragrant salt-and-pepper eggplant. When it came to dessert I'd been unable to decide, so in the end I'd made two of Nadine Ingram's chiffon cakes—black sesame chiffon and elderflower chiffon with crème fraîche icing. Normally my friends are such piglets—and me such an over-feeder—that they've eaten too much of the first two courses to touch dessert. At this dinner, though, drunk on the excite-ment of finally being reunited, both cakes were devoured within minutes.

Cooking for others without the intention to impress or outdo but only as an expression of love can be a beautifully transformative thing. That dinner was the first time the Ginger had seen me in full flight—hosting and cooking and entertaining. He saw my friends sitting at my table and he saw me letting them know they were seen, they were important, and they were loved.

The following night saw the Ginger and me go out for dinner for the first time, to Bar Vincent. Perched up at the bar, we devoured spring vegetables in buffalo curd and panzerotti alla norma. It was over our mains of gnudi di cime di rapa and nettle risotto that we both started to cry as we leaned in and confessed we had begun to fall for each other. We finished with the most perfect apple and almond galette, and the walk home, which should have taken fifteen minutes, ended up taking us close to an hour as we sang and danced our way through the streets of Darlinghurst. We were practically vomiting rainbows.

There is no better feeling than the pure, unadulterated joy of realising you are falling in love with someone. And that they, in return, are falling in love with you.

There are days when your heart feels settled, as though its wounds have finally healed. But there are days when those wounds still feel raw, as if they are gaping open for the world to see.

Early one morning, after a night of little to no sleep, I woke at the Ginger's house with what I can only describe as a vulnerability hangover. Anxiety rising, heart racing, I stared at the ceiling, spiralling. It was the unwelcome familiarity of my Easter panic attack all over again.

Sensing my distress, the Ginger woke, reached for me and, like a lighthouse guiding me to shore, he pulled me out of my head and grounded me in the present—a present in which a pied currawong was offering its early morning song. The Ginger began to rattle off an unexpected wealth of bird facts. He told me that the pied currawong is often confused with a magpie, but you can tell the two apart because the currawong is almost entirely black and has a distinctive yellow eye. He told me that it is the females who build the nests, and that their melodious call—*curra-wong, curra-wong*—is how they got their name.

I knew I loved him then.

Falling in love again was exciting, but it was scary too. At first I found myself questioning if I was falling in love with him or falling in love with the person I became when I was with him. Someone comfortable in her own skin, someone proud of who she was and what she had overcome. Someone who had grown and was continuing to grow. Someone who had gone to the core of herself to find peace and understanding. Someone who had finally found happiness, found meaning and found heart-bursting joy-filled love. Because in finally being able to fully recognise myself, in liking myself, I had also learned to love myself.

But I was beginning to feel deeply uncomfortable about having someone else show me love. I wasn't sure I could trust it, trust myself. It was as if I feared getting too comfortable, too used to having someone, in case their love was suddenly snatched away.

I decided to see the Oracle again.

She told me that couple development is like child development and now, in our six months of whirlwind romance, the Ginger and I had become attached. My anxiety was born of the feeling that I had something to lose, and the fear I felt at the prospect of losing him was overwhelming.

My anxiety was stemming from the anxious attachment style I had developed in childhood. But I wanted to change that. The words of Natasha Lunn, in her book *Conversations on Love*, struck a chord: 'I still believed the act of showing yourself fully to a new person was a risk, but the risk of not doing so—of never being seen, of never expressing needs, of never giving and accepting real love—was far greater.'

I had never been more sure of anyone or anything. Never been more convinced of someone's profound and lasting impact on me, on who I was, the joy I felt, and the person I wanted to be for myself—and for him too.

I realised that it takes time to accommodate being loved like this. A love that didn't feel like being scared or intimidated or controlled. A love that didn't require me to look after anyone without asking for anything for myself. In believing that the Ginger loved me, I had to finally believe that I was loveable. The knot I'd had in my stomach all my life was loosening as I was learning to love someone without losing myself. The Oracle was encouraging me to swallow. I was opening myself up to triumph and joy.

My voyage of self-discovery had taught me that, no matter what happened between the Ginger and me, I would be okay. Because I had myself to return to.

The Ginger radiated joy from every fibre of his being. He was someone who was hungry for every experience in life. He was passionately curious. He was fascinated by people, and by the world around him. He was engaged and engaging. He had the ability to make me laugh every single day. He loved to read, and he read widely. And, most incredibly, I had finally found someone who would happily sit in silence with me, each of us with a book in hand. He exerted both a calming force and a magnetic attraction. He didn't do things by halves. He loved to sing, without realising he was doing it, particularly when cooking. He would text me when we weren't together to tell me to go outside and look at the moon. He loved native plants. He adored birds, particularly the rainbow lorikeets that turned up on his balcony each day to pester him until he fed them. He lived and breathed the ocean, swimming, surfing or free-diving. He loved underwater creatures and would never eat them or any other animal. He loved to be kissed on the cheek, or on the forehead. He loved having his head rubbed and his chest hair stroked. He unashamedly wore socks with Birkenstocks and somehow made it seem fashionable. His brain was full of facts, bubbling with ideas. He showed me ways to touch without words—by opening the car door for me, by picking me flowers, by making my bed. He was hungry for wild adventure days and satiated by days spent doing nothing. For mornings in bed with the *Good Weekend* quiz, and for evenings spent watching *Spicks and Specks*, yelling guesses at the television. He would end each day, even the toughest of days, by asking me what my highlight was, reminding me to always find beauty amidst any pain, to find light in the dark.

He had an insatiable appetite not only for life but for food. Just like my grandmother had, he expressed his enjoyment of every mouthful audibly. He was an incredible cook, and he learned to make the perfect hard-boiled egg—for me. When someone hard-boils eggs for you, you know they love you and it is impossible not to love them in return.

On my daily call with Grampy, I told him about the Ginger and how he made me feel, and how I felt about him. Grampy asked me if I had told him I was in love with him yet, and I admitted that I hadn't. 'Well, what are you waiting for?' he replied.

It was 16 October. We were walking through the aisles of Coles in Bondi Junction and I was bursting out of my skin. I could no longer contain my feelings for this man. Stopping in front of the caster sugar, I said three words I had never expected to say so soon.

'I love you.'

The Ginger stopped walking and looked at me, then he quickly replied, as if rushing to get it out, 'I love you too.'

The words felt strange, foreign, at first. I didn't know how this had happened, but it felt like something *big*.

We were in *love*.

He burst into tears, and we spent the rest of our supermarket shop walking around in a daze. He was still crying when we reached the checkout.

We went downstairs to the bottle shop and purchased a bottle of champagne. We decided to treat ourselves to an expensive vintage, and when the saleswoman came to open the locked cabinet to retrieve our choice, she asked what the occasion was. We explained to her that we had just told each other we loved each other, and she rolled her eyes. The woman at the register, on the other hand, noted that the champagne had been bottled in the same year that she'd met her husband. She burst into tears when we told her the reason we were purchasing it, and she wished us a happy life together.

My stomach was doing somersaults, so I told the Ginger I needed to stop on the way home to buy some ginger beer. I was on my way back to the car when, halfway across the road, I saw him in the front seat, still crying. Distracted, I tripped over my own feet, falling face-first into the bitumen. The ginger beer went flying, smashing as it landed, and glass became embedded in my right arm. My dress was shredded. There was blood everywhere.

I looked up, bewildered, to see the Ginger stepping from the car.

'Oh, Charlotte,' he sighed. Then, like the romantic lead in a Hollywood film, he carefully picked the glass from my arm then removed his shirt and used it to staunch the bleeding before carrying me to the safety of the footpath.

My accident was what we needed to shock us back into ourselves. I stopped feeling nauseated, he stopped crying, and instead we laughed hysterically.

The next day, Ken took us out on his boss's boat. It could not have been a more perfect Sydney day, and I could not have been happier. As we cruised under the Harbour Bridge and I looked over at the Ginger lovingly, I realised just how far I had come in the two years since, on another boat ride, I had made the decision to leave my marriage. The life of adventure and discovery and possibility and happiness I had dreamed of that day had become my reality.

The Ginger and I were beginning our relationship with an immense amount of respect for one another and, crucially, we were building a relationship that was strong on communication, playfulness and trust.

When I got home that night, he sent me a beautiful message.

> I'm so grateful for you. I'm so grateful for this weekend. I am so grateful for your patience. I'm so grateful for your overwhelming joy. I'm so grateful for your ridiculous brain. I'm weirdly grateful for some, but not all, of the tougher things that have happened to you that have made you who you are. I'm so grateful for the work I've done on myself to both feel like I might deserve something like this, and to be open to recognising it when it comes my way and not be scared of it. I was being honest when I said you both excite and intimidate the fuck out of me. I'm excited and intimidated by what I feel like we could accomplish together. I think you're going to inspire and require me to be the best version of myself, which is mainly exciting but also a little bit terrifying.

I now see my twenties as a time of agonising impatience. A decade of trying desperately to understand myself and those around me, of finally moving beyond the fantasy of what life should be, what a partner should be, and getting to know instead the person I was underneath the masks I wore in an attempt to please and impress others. I was finding my place in the world and, in doing so, found self-acceptance. As I entered my thirties, I was embracing new beginnings— navigating the unseen and the not-yet-understood. I was embracing the unknown, resisting my urge to control so that I could keep myself open to discovery. Open to loving deeply. To living fearlessly.

In her speech at my wedding, my mama had referenced Kahlil Gibran's 'On Marriage', speaking about how couples needed to establish separateness to foster togetherness. I hadn't understood what she meant then, but I did now. I no longer expected a relationship to be my whole world. I was cultivating separateness, a sense of self, that in turn nurtured our togetherness. 'All companionship,' Rilke writes in *Letters to a Young Poet*, 'can consist in only the strengthening of neighbouring solitudes.'

I now chose to live in the skin I was in. I buttered bread without guilt. I no longer wore make-up. I cooked and ate with abandon. I was in awe of my curves. I didn't need to drink to forget anymore. I wanted to remember *everything*. To soak it all in.

My inner voice told me that I was safe now. I had found myself. I was no longer on my own as, in so many ways, I had returned home. I might get lost along the way occasionally, but I would find myself again. I'd always find myself because I knew myself now. I wanted to sit with myself, bake myself focaccia and pour myself a wine. I wanted to give my heart back to itself. I wanted to marvel at my brain and my body. I wanted to feast on my life.

Because I knew now that I could feel everything and not only survive, but thrive.

freeze

At the bottom of every frozen heart there is a drop or two of love—just enough to feed the birds.

HENRY MILLER, *TROPIC OF CANCER*

It was a warm Monday morning, but I was feeling cold. I could not comprehend what the Ginger was saying to me: that he could no longer see an 'us', that he did not see a future with me. I was trying to hold myself together, trying not to vomit.

'I will be okay, I will be okay, I will be okay.' I repeated the words over and over, willing them to be true. Willing myself to accept an ending not of my making, with so much out of my sphere of control. Life is not linear, I reminded myself. Life is messy. It is imperfect.

The Ginger left, and I began to weep: for him, for myself—for us. After such an intense love, the loss, the grief, was profound, earth-shattering. I so desperately *needed* him; I so desperately *wanted* him. Every part of my being ached for him; for his touch, his warmth, his scent, his voice. But I know now that some loves, though beautiful, are only fleeting.

The plane landed at Coolangatta airport and Mama was there to meet me. She pulled me into her and wrapped her arms around me. I fell into her embrace. Instantly I was reminded that one of my greatest loves is eternal. Mama led me to the car and turned on the seat warmers and on the way home she serenaded me with songs from my childhood—Carole King, Joni Mitchell, Cat Stevens, Carly Simon, Mama Cass. But she knew I was heartsick, knew that she could not sing away this pain. The faint memory of her own lost loves, long since passed, reminded her of this, and she cried as she sang for me.

Home. I was craving salt and starch; I needed comfort food from my childhood. Pa didn't say much, but he understood. He brought me warm bowlfuls of mashed potato, pumpkin, peas and thick onion gravy, and Mama fed me. I felt raw, vulnerable. Grampy arrived and I curled up on his lap like a child; I was bone-weary.

Mum made cups of tea; she braided my hair; and she checked on me throughout the night to make sure I was sleeping. And when she saw I was not, she told me that I was not alone, that she was there.

I had done so much work with the Oracle that I had been able to feel it *all* in my relationship with the Ginger—absolute rapture and, now, indescribable pain. What I'd learned had been a gift. It was the gift of being able to feel everything and know I would survive. To grieve. To remember. To want. To hope. To find. To love. To experience joy. To falter. To lose. To ache. To learn. To strive. To seek. To accomplish. To begin again.

Because with every ending comes a beginning. The opportunity to re-evaluate, realign and re-centre yourself. To rediscover *your* standards. *Your* worth. *Your* beliefs. *Your* intentions. *Your* needs. *Your* desires. *Your* strength. *Your* grit. *Your* determination.

Life is not linear. Life is messy. It is imperfect. But I know, too, that life can be beautiful. The Ginger has shown me that.

And I know that our hearts did love. And I know that when I hear the song of the pied currawong, that's now so bitter and sweet, the memory of him will sing to me, a heartbreak of my very own.

fusion

Every kind of new music was created by a fusion of different styles because to move on and find something new you have to allow all the influences within yourself a voice.

VOLKER BERTELMANN, INTERVIEW WITH *THE RUMPUS*

It's serendipitous that my writing of this book began, and now ends, with heartbreak.

I know now that this heartbreak and many other immeasurable collective moments have formed and transformed me, shaped me into the many versions of myself—some familiar and some foreign. For I was not the same woman at 29 that I was at 19, and I am not the same version of myself now, at 31. I am a fusion of all these versions of me—a single entity.

Because I know that if the past few years have taught me anything, it's that the relationship you have with yourself is the single most important relationship you will ever have. Now it's time for me to remember how to hold onto myself when someone else has let me go.

It's serendipitous as well that my writing began, and now ends, with an egg.

In my saddest moments, a single egg, eaten daily, sustained me and nourished me. I understood that an egg embodied a rebirth for me, whereby I could gently crack the egg open from the inside—using an intrinsic force, a learned strength.

It was a rebirth in which the lucent warmth silently seeped through the cracks to chase away the shadows, to show me that I was not broken. A light enticing me forward—encouraging me to begin again.

As I write these final words I am sitting with the sunshine of a soft-boiled egg, served in an egg cup, toast soldiers on the side dripping in butter, and a warm mug of French Earl Grey tea nestled in between my hands.

feed

Keep it simple, everything will turn out just fine.

LAURIE COLWIN, *MORE HOME COOKING*

how to boil an egg

Boiled eggs nourished me when I couldn't nourish myself.

To make them, fill a small saucepan with cold tap water and place over medium heat. Gently lower your free-range eggs into the water, and when it begins to simmer, start your timer for the perfect boiled eggs. For soft runny yolks, simmer in the water for 4 minutes. For semi-firm yolks and hard whites, keep the eggs simmering for 5 minutes. For hard boiled, my favourite, simmer the eggs for 8 minutes.

Empty the boiling water out of the saucepan, shake the saucepan to crack the shell and place under cold running water. This will shock the white and your eggshell will peel off like snakeskin.

I love to serve soft-boiled runny eggs in an egg cup with soldiers dripping in butter. But I *really* love to eat hard-boiled eggs whole, drowned in sea salt flakes and freshly ground black pepper, served with a little drizzle of extra virgin olive oil poured over the top.

David Lovett's focaccia

In the first lockdown, unlike what appeared to be the rest of the world, I never made sourdough bread. I struggled to maintain a starter—not being able to feed myself, I couldn't bring myself to feed it. But I did bake tray after tray of focaccia, and became obsessed with perfecting it, even throughout the great supermarket yeast shortage of 2020. I tried countless recipes in my search for perfection. Some called for the seemingly rogue addition of potato, some begged you not to knead, others compelled you to do so forever. There were recipes that called for your dough to be refrigerated and there was even that infamous one that asks you to leave your dough to ferment at room temperature for twelve to fourteen hours. How absurd.

I now realise there is just one focaccia recipe you must memorise and bake for the rest of your life. It is my friend David Lovett's focaccia, and it is a masterpiece. You only need to use plain flour, and you don't need to waste your time with strange ingredients or two days of proofing. And you can simply enhance it with any additions of your choosing.

I serve it alongside a caprese salad, which I make by combining punnets of halved ripe cherry tomatoes with clouds of creamy stracciatella and a couple of handfuls of torn fresh basil leaves on a large serving platter. I season it well with sea salt and black pepper, and then drizzle olive oil all over. It's the ultimate pairing.

350 ml tepid water
10 g dried yeast
10 g caster sugar
500 g plain flour, sifted
2 teaspoons fine sea salt
Extra virgin olive oil
Polenta, for dusting
Sea salt flakes, to season
250 g punnet cherry tomatoes, halved
2 tablespoons rosemary leaves

Place the water, yeast and sugar in the bowl of your electric mixer fitted with a dough hook and mix to combine. Add the sifted flour and fine sea salt, then mix, scraping down the side occasionally with a spatula to incorporate all the flour, until a sticky dough forms (8–10 minutes). This is a wet dough, so be careful not to add more flour than the recipe calls for. The ratios are key.

Lightly oil a deep baking tray (mine is around 20 × 30 cm) with the extra virgin olive oil and dust with the polenta. Using a pastry scraper, scrape the dough into a ball and place in your tray.

Rub a tablespoon of extra virgin olive oil all over the dough ball and set aside to prove until doubled in size (20–30 minutes; the warmer and more humid the room, the quicker it will prove).

Stretch the dough to fill the tray (it should be soft and pillowy; be gentle so as to keep as much air in the dough as possible). Using both hands, lift the dough from underneath and gently stretch and pull it lengthways, then sideways. If it doesn't quite reach the edges, that's fine. As it proves the second time, it will expand further. Drizzle 1½ tablespoons of extra virgin olive oil over the dough and leave to prove for another 10–14 minutes. It will continue to gently rise.

Preheat your oven to 240°C. Using all your fingers (but not thumbs) on both hands, make deep indents in the dough with your fingertips, then drizzle another 1½ tablespoons of extra virgin olive oil all over. Set aside to prove for a further 10–12 minutes. It will rise even more.

Now, when it comes to flavouring your focaccia, the choice is yours. You can leave the homemade dough to shine, serving it with just extra virgin olive oil and sea salt flakes. You could add a sprinkling of oregano leaves, too. You can make what David calls the 'Bunnings focaccia' by gently pressing a packet of plain thin pork sausages and 2 teaspoons of rosemary leaves into your focaccia. You can then serve it with sautéed onions and your favourite sauce.

But my go-to is pressing halved cherry tomatoes, cut side up, into the dough, and scattering 2 tablespoons of rosemary over the top.

After adding your flavourings, drizzle on another 1½ tablespoons of extra virgin olive oil and set aside to prove until the dough is popping over the edge of the tray and the oil is about to overflow. Depending on your tray size, you want to aim for your dough to be about 3 cm deep by this point.

Season generously with 2–3 teaspoons of sea salt flakes. Bake until the focaccia is deep golden and sounds hollow when tapped (12–15 minutes). Add one final, generous drizzle of extra virgin olive oil as soon as the focaccia comes out of the oven, then rest in the tray for about 5 minutes. Turn out on a wire rack to cool for 20–30 minutes.

Serves 6–8.

Mama's spinach pie

This is the recipe for my mama's spinach pie. The pie that I baked to feel like I was home. The pie that with every mouthful made me feel like my mama was holding me, feeding me, healing me.

There're a few key things she swears by, and that's using silverbeet leaves instead of spinach leaves (and yes, we still call it spinach pie and not silverbeet pie), Dodoni feta (she says it's the saltiest) and Antoniou fillo pastry (which you can find in the fridge of your supermarket).

2 bunches of silverbeet

1 brown onion

2 spring onions

Olive oil, for cooking

5 large free-range eggs

250 g Dodoni feta

250 g fresh ricotta, drained

A bunch of dill, finely chopped

Freshly ground black pepper, to taste

250 g unsalted butter, melted

375 g Antoniou fillo pastry

Preheat the oven to 180°C. Wash the silverbeet and strip the leaves from the stalks. In batches, steam the silverbeet leaves till soft. Leave to cool and drain. Once cool, using your hands, squeeze the moisture from the silverbeet and tear or cut into squares. Set aside to cool.

Peel the onion and cut it into eighths lengthways, so you have long wedges. Cut up the spring onions into 2 cm lengths. Add the olive oil to a frypan on low heat and caramelise the onion and spring onions for around 10 minutes. Set aside to cool.

Beat the eggs well in a large bowl, then crumble in the feta. Crumble well so you don't have any big chunks, then mix in the ricotta and dill too.

Let it sit to marinate until the onion mixture is cool. (Make sure the silverbeet and onion are both cool before adding them to the egg and cheese mixture, so the eggs don't cook.) Now add the cooled onion and silverbeet to the bowl, season with pepper to taste, and leave to sit while you prepare the fillo.

Using a pastry brush, grease the bottom of your dish (I use Mum's special dish but you can use any round 24 cm pie dish) with some of the melted butter. Line the base and sides with two layers of fillo pastry, brushing on more butter between each layer. Then add another two layers in the opposite direction. The pastry sheets should hang over the side of the dish. Repeat, buttering between sheets, until you have used all but two sheets of fillo. You will use these to make the top of the pie.

Now, pour the egg, cheese and greens mixture into the middle of the dish and spread it out evenly. Then, get your remaining two sheets of fillo pastry, butter them, fold them in half and place in the middle of the dish. Fold over the excess pastry that has been hanging over the side and, working layer to layer, and buttering each layer as you go, fold and gently pull them into the middle of the dish to form a top layer sealing the pie.

Bake until the pastry is golden brown, around an hour. Serves 8.

whole baked snapper

Sometimes all I want to eat is a piece of fish cooked on the bone, and this whole baked snapper fits the bill perfectly. Not only is it incredibly simple to prepare and absolutely delicious, it also looks ridiculously impressive placed on the table, having been baked on a bed of lemon, its insides stuffed with butter and dill.

Preheat the oven to 200°C. Line a large baking tray, big enough to fit your fish (mine is normally a 1 kg whole snapper which has been cleaned, gutted and scaled by my fishmonger—you can ask yours to do this too), with baking paper.

Score your fish on both sides with a few deep slits, rubbing olive oil, salt and pepper inside and out—this helps you to control the fish peeling apart as it cooks. Place half a whole lemon, cut into 5 mm slices, some thin slices of salted butter as well as four sprigs of dill inside the fish cavity. Arrange slices of the remaining lemon half and some more butter slices on the top and underside of the fish. Transfer to the oven and bake until the snapper is cooked through— about 30–35 minutes. You can tell your fish is cooked through by piercing the thickest part of the fish with a fork. The fish will come apart easily (without resistance) when it is cooked, and will have lost its translucent appearance.

FEED

To serve, I tend to steam some greens like asparagus or broccolini, then sauté a little butter in a small frypan and add the steamed greens into the butter to coat them. Sometimes I also steam some little chat potatoes and cover them in some more sautéed butter, and toss with some finely chopped dill. Otherwise, the 'salad' on page 294 pairs perfectly too.

Serves 4.

spaghetti vongole

This recipe is ridiculously easy to make, and even more wonderful to devour. It should serve four, but often I find it is the perfect amount for a pair of hungry lovers.

Extra virgin olive oil

250 g punnet of cherry tomatoes

Sea salt flakes, for seasoning

4 garlic cloves, crushed

400 g dried spaghetti

150 ml dry white wine

1 kg fresh vongole (or pipis), from the refrigerator of your fishmonger

½ bunch of flat-leaf parsley, chopped

To begin, pour a glug of extra virgin olive oil, empty the punnet of tomatoes and sprinkle a generous pinch of sea salt flakes into a large heavy-based cast-iron pot. Let the tomatoes cook low and slow for 40 or so minutes until they blister and start to fall apart, beginning to make a sauce when stirred. Stir through the garlic. Taste, and season with additional salt if required. (I find it is always required.)

Cook the spaghetti in a saucepan of boiling salted water, according to the packet instructions, until al dente. Reserve ½ cup of pasta water when draining.

Add the white wine (usually I add whatever I am drinking) and the vongole to the tomato sauce, cover with a lid and cook on high heat until the vongole open, about 3 minutes. Discard any unopened shells. Add the pasta, reserved pasta water and parsley, and toss to combine.

Serve immediately, pouring a drizzle of olive oil over each bowl—and make sure you have an extra bowl on your table to place those empty shells in.

Pa's pesto

I love pesto with every fibre of my being. It takes me back to my childhood, when I would be surrounded by Pa's sweet-smelling basil plants. He would often make chicken pesto pasta when I had study sleepovers with friends, and we would eat it by the bowlful—hot or cold. He always had a stash of pesto in the freezer and when I moved out on my own, I found solace in having a freezerful for myself, too. I divide its velvety green goodness into individual portions in zip-lock bags, named and dated, then add it from frozen to a tablespoon or two of reserved pasta cooking water and a handful of freshly grated Parmigiano to create a delightfully silky sauce.

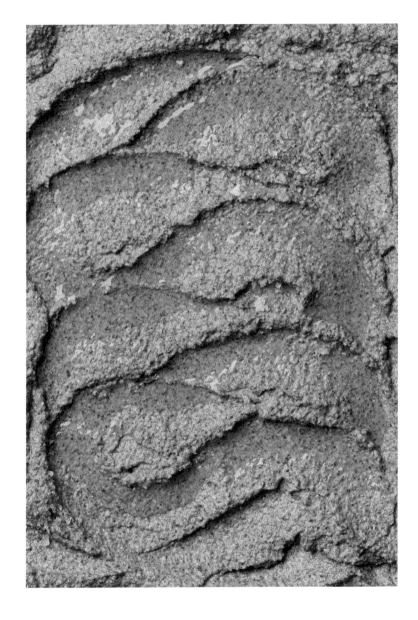

1 bunch of basil leaves
120 g baby spinach leaves
30 g pine nuts, lightly toasted
1 garlic clove, peeled
Pinch of sea salt flakes
80 g freshly grated Parmigiano Reggiano
Extra virgin olive oil

To make the pesto, combine the basil, spinach, pine nuts, garlic and salt in a food processor. Pulse until a smooth paste forms. Add the Parmigiano and pulse until combined. With the motor running on its lowest speed, drizzle in the extra virgin olive oil until it binds and you create a smooth sauce.

This recipe makes ½ cup pesto, which I divide into 4 individual portions stored in zip-lock bags.

ricotta and pesto ravioli in brown butter sage sauce

This was the very first meal I ever made for the Ginger, serving the tender and translucent pasta pillows in a sauce of sautéed crispy sage and browned butter.

Pasta

300 g Tipo 00 flour
3 large free-range eggs

Filling

1 batch of Pa's pesto (page 260)
250 g fresh ricotta, drained
Sea salt flakes
Freshly ground black pepper

Sauce

120 g unsalted butter
10 g punnet of fresh sage leaves
Parmigiano Reggiano, freshly grated, to serve

Make the pasta by combining the flour and eggs in the bowl of your electric mixer fitted with a dough hook.

Knead on medium speed for 10 minutes until you have a soft dough—when you gently press your finger into it, the dough will spring back.

If you do not have an electric mixer, it is time for an arm workout. Pour the flour onto a clean, dry work surface and make a well in the middle. Pour in the eggs and, using a fork, gently whisk. Using the same fork, slowly incorporate the flour into the well, working clockwise, until a clumpy dough forms. Forego the fork; now is the time to use lightly floured hands. Slowly bring the dough together, forming a ball, and knead for 8–10 minutes until you can gently press your finger into it, and the dough springs back.

In both instances—mixer or handmade—gently flatten your dough ball into a disc and wrap in plastic wrap. Leave it in a cool, dry place for 30 minutes, while you make your filling.

To make the ravioli filling, make a batch of Pa's pesto, stir in the ricotta, season with salt and pepper and set aside.

Separate your rested dough into four equal portions, each wrapped in plastic wrap, ready for rolling out. Working with one dough quarter at a time to ensure it doesn't dry out, and using a pasta machine, roll each portion of dough into a sheet around 1.2 mm thick. You may need two sets of hands here, and you may need to add a little extra showering of flour to each quarter to stop it sticking as you roll. I love to make the dough with my guests when they have arrived and have a wine in hand. It is something that we can all do together.

Place each rolled sheet on a lightly floured work surface. You can be precise, measuring your sheets with a ruler and cutting them into 7 cm squares. But I often find freehand works just as well too. Place a tablespoon of the pesto and ricotta filling in the middle of each pasta square. Dip your finger in water and run it around the edge of the squares to help them stick. Fold one corner of each square over to the opposite side to form a triangle. Seal by pressing down on all the edges, removing the air with your index fingers. Then run a knife or ribbed pastry cutter along the edges to seal completely. Place your ravioli on a floured board or tea towel, and repeat with the remaining dough portions until you have used all your filling.

To make the sauce, brown the butter and sage leaves in a heavy-based cast-iron pot over medium heat until the butter is nutty and the sage leaves crispy. Season with salt. Remove from the heat.

Cook the ravioli in a large pot of salted simmering, not boiling, water till they float to the surface, around 3 minutes each, transferring them to the sauce pot with a slotted spoon. You may need to do this in batches. Reserve ¼ cup of pasta water when you've finished.

Add the pasta water to the pot, tossing gently to coat the ravioli in the nutty, buttery, crispy sauce. Serve immediately with the freshly grated Parmigiano Reggiano.

Serves 2.

eggplant pasta

I have always been extremely fond of eggplant, gobbling it up in the form of my mama's moussaka, or painstakingly layering it in a parmigiana, or marinating it in miso, or coating it in cornflour, frying it and tossing it in allspice, sea salt and white pepper.

But it is this simple combination I love the most. It's what I make after a mammoth day of writing when I am too tired to think of anything else to cook. The quantities of ingredients of course depend on how many are eating, or if I want there to be any leftovers to reheat for lunch the next day.

First, I chop an eggplant into chunky 2 cm cubes. Then I sauté it in a frypan with copious amounts of olive oil and minced cloves of garlic (a lot of them), and leave it to stew until it has completely softened. Oh, and don't forget a generous sprinkling of sea salt flakes. I am a salt fiend after all.

While the eggplant is cooking, I chuck a tin of Mutti roma tomatoes in a separate frypan, and heat them up with another glug of extra virgin olive oil and . . . sea salt. Are you sensing a pattern here?

To bring it all together, I cook my chosen pasta until al dente, normally short and ribbed—I love a casarecce, creste

di gallo (looks like a rooster's head), penne or rigatoni—
in a pot of salted boiling water according to its packet
instructions, reserving some pasta water before draining.
I then combine the cooked pasta, pasta water and eggplant
with the tomato sauce, mixing so the pasta and eggplant
are covered entirely.

I then cover everything with some freshly grated
Parmigiano, probably another pinch (or two, oops) of
sea salt, and devour it, always eating way more than my
stomach allows because I can't help but come back for more.
It's really so very good.

my comforting lasagne'

I recognise this recipe is not traditional, by any means.
It features a sauce that has more liquid than some might
like and a bechamel that my nanny taught me how to
make by sight rather than measurement (which also made
it incredibly difficult to convert here). But this is a recipe
that is full of my whole heart and one that I have curated,
perfected and fawned over for many years.

The highest praise of all was in a letter my husband
wrote to me after we had separated, which he ended by
saying 'P.S. I think you now finally make a better lasagne
than me'. And now, you can too.

Sauce

3 celery stalks, grated

3 large carrots, grated

1 brown onion, diced

3 zucchinis, grated

Extra virgin olive oil

500 g pork mince

500 g beef mince

1 cup dry red wine

Sea salt flakes and freshly ground black pepper

800 g tinned whole peeled tomatoes (I prefer Mutti brand)

140 g tomato paste (I prefer Mutti brand)

700 ml tomato passata (I prefer Mutti brand)

1 cup full-cream milk

1 tablespoon oregano leaves

4 garlic cloves, crushed

Pasta

2 batches of pasta dough (see page 265)

Bechamel

4 tablespoons unsalted butter

150 g plain flour

1.5 litres full-cream milk

1 teaspoon ground nutmeg

200 g Parmigiano Reggiano, grated, plus extra for topping and serving

150 g mozzarella, grated, for topping

To make the sauce, sauté the celery, carrot, onion and zucchini in a heavy-based cast-iron pot with olive oil on medium heat until softened. Add the pork and beef minces and break them into small, pea-sized pieces with your wooden spoon. Brown slightly and add your red wine. Season with salt and pepper. Continue to cook the meat until it browns, and the wine reduces. Add the tomatoes, tomato paste and passata. Stir. Cook till everything bubbles, then turn the heat down to low. Add the milk, oregano and garlic as well as some more salt and pepper if needed. Cook, stirring occasionally, for a minimum of 6 hours.

Once your sauce has been made, make the pasta using the pasta instructions in the ravioli recipe, following the instructions until your dough is flattened into a disc and covered in plastic wrap. Be sure to make a double batch. Once you've finished, leave in a cool dark place while you make your bechamel.

Preheat the oven to 180°C and prepare your chosen baking dish by drizzling the bottom with some extra virgin olive oil.

To make the bechamel, melt the butter in a large saucepan over medium heat. Add the flour and whisk constantly for 3 or so minutes, until the mixture begins to cook and form bubbles. Gradually add the milk, whisking constantly to avoid any lumps forming. Slowly bring to the boil, continuing to stir as the sauce thickens, for about 8 or so minutes. You want a beautifully thick but still slightly runny bechamel, like a gravy, that coats the back of a spoon. Once you have reached that consistency, stir through the nutmeg and Parmigiano, seasoning with salt and pepper. Note that the bechamel can become too thick if it is left for too long while you are layering. If you see this happening to you, simply add some more milk and stir to thin it slightly.

Now is the time to roll out the lasagne sheets by dividing the rested dough into 4 equal parts and rolling each sheet with a pasta roller to approximately 1.2 mm thick. You may need two sets of hands here and may need to add a little extra showering of flour to each quarter to stop it sticking. I normally store my rolled sheets on my portable clothes drying rack from Ikea, or on the backs of my dining chairs (thanks to my tiny kitchen), but if I am making them with friends, I simply add them to my baking dish and layer as I go.

To construct the lasagne, lightly line the base of your baking dish with some of the sauce and another drizzle of extra virgin olive oil. Place a layer of pasta sheets on top, then spread one-third of your remaining sauce over the pasta, then one third of the bechamel and a drizzle of extra virgin olive oil. Repeat this layering process until you reach your final layer of pasta, which you will top with bechamel and a sprinkling of extra Parmigiano, and then cover with the mozzarella. Bake in the oven for 45 minutes until it is bubbling and golden and you are salivating at the thought!

Patience will reward you though. Once you remove your lasagne from the oven, leave it to rest for 10–20 minutes before serving. This will allow the layers to settle into themselves.

Scatter with a little more grated Parmigiano and serve. Serves 8–10.

vodka pasta

The beauty of this dish lies in its speed and simplicity.
It features ingredients that are often found in my pantry,
and might be staples of your own too. Vodka pasta is
a recipe that consumed the appetites of many during
lockdown. A lot of variations feature the addition of chilli
and pancetta and encourage you to use rigatoni or penne
pasta. But I prefer the bones of this sauce to be bare, and
for it to be served with an even shorter pasta shape, like
cavatelli or small shells. Threesomes aside, it feels like a
hug in a bowl.

Extra virgin olive oil

1 French shallot (eschalot), finely diced

4 garlic cloves, crushed

140 g double concentrate tomato paste (I prefer Mutti brand)

3 tablespoons vodka

500 g short dried pasta like cavatelli or small shells

240 ml thickened cream

100 g Parmigiano Reggiano, finely grated, plus extra to serve

Sea salt flakes, for seasoning

Chilli flakes, to serve

For three generous portions, with the possibility of a fourth, heat the extra virgin olive oil in a large heavy-based cast-iron pot over medium heat. Add the shallot and garlic and cook, stirring, until they are softened and your kitchen is fragrant with possibility. Chuck in the tomato paste and cook, stirring, until it becomes rich and red. There's a lot that may be stuck to the bottom of your pot and so add the vodka (I just get the cheapest no-brand from the bottom shelf) to deglaze the pan, scraping every last morsel that's stuck, and reduce the heat to low.

Cook the pasta in a pot of salted boiling water according to the packet instructions, reserving ¼ cup of the pasta water.

Bring the sauce to a gentle simmer over medium heat and add the cream, Parmigiano and reserved pasta water. Add the pasta to your pot of sauce, stirring constantly until it is well coated. Season with salt and serve immediately in bowls topped with extra freshly grated Parmigiano and the chilli flakes.

the perfect pasta sauce'

I refer to this recipe, inspired by the Italian cooking legend Marcella Hazan, as my blood, bones and butter.

The sauce is terrifyingly good—buttery, sweet, moreish—and there's no guilt because you have made it yourself, and because it is so lip-smackingly simple.

You simply put four ingredients—a peeled and halved brown onion, a tin of whole peeled tomatoes, a generous stick of butter, and a handful of sea salt flakes—into a heavy-based cast-iron pan. No slicing or dicing required. You just break up the tomatoes using the back of a wooden spoon. Then you bring them to a slow but steady simmer and let them cook for 45 minutes. The result is buttery perfection.

To serve, I cook spaghetti in salted boiling water according to its packet instructions. And I am talking about stock standard spaghetti—no. 5 minimum—none of that angel hair bullshit. Sometimes I reserve a little pasta water and I combine the water with the sauce and the spaghetti, sprinkling some finely chopped parsley and freshly grated Parmigiano over the top. As with Pa's pesto recipe, I like to freeze any remaining sauce into individually portioned zip-lock bags for when I want something comforting but feel too exhausted to cook.

FEED

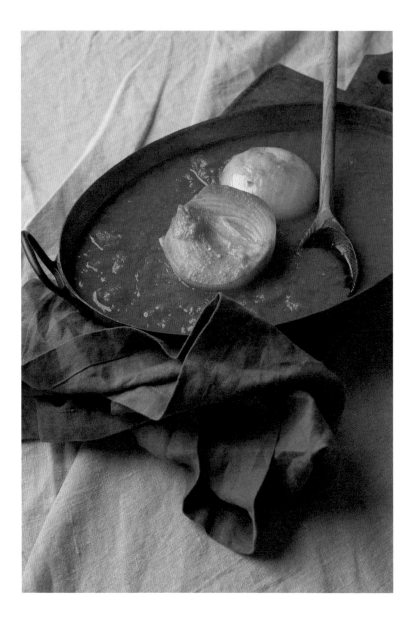

prawn wonton noodle soup

One of my biggest cravings during lockdown was wonton noodle soup. The broth can be made in advance and frozen. The dumplings can be made and eaten fresh, or frozen on a baking tray with a 1 cm gap left between each to stop the wrappers sticking together. You can then transfer the frozen dumplings to a container or zip-lock bag for better use of your freezer space.

Broth

1.5–2 kg free-range, organic whole chicken
1 kg smoked ham hock
4 tablespoons dried shrimp
1 tablespoon black peppercorns
2 tablespoons sea salt flakes
1 tablespoon caster sugar
1 bunch of spring onions
10 garlic cloves, peeled and halved
8 cm piece of ginger, cut into thick chunks

Wontons

250 g raw peeled prawns, butterflied
1 teaspoon sea salt flakes
1 teaspoon caster sugar
½ teaspoon sesame oil, plus extra for drizzling
270 g packet of wonton wrappers, refrigerated (I prefer Double
    Merinos brand)

To serve

375 g fresh wonton noodles
2 bunches of gai lan
Spring onion, chopped
Coriander, chopped

Remove the chicken from its packaging. Fill a large stock pot around three-quarters full with water (you will need enough room to add the chicken without it overflowing) and bring it to the boil. Using a large pair of tongs, carefully lower your whole chicken into the boiling water and blanch for 3 minutes, before lifting it out and rinsing under cold water. (Blanching the chicken ensures you get rid of any impurities and end up with a beautifully clear stock.)

Preheat the oven to 160°C.

Place the chicken in a large heavy-based cast-iron pot (or a large pot with a lid that is oven safe). Adjust your oven racks if needed, to allow for the height of your pot. Add the ham hock, dried shrimp, peppercorns, sea salt, sugar, whole spring onions, garlic and ginger. Fill with water, leaving a 3 cm gap at the top, and put the lid on. Note that the pot will be quite heavy at this stage, so be careful when transferring it to the oven. Leave it to cook low and slow for 6 hours or so.

While the broth is cooking, marinate the peeled and butterflied prawns in a small bowl with the sea salt, sugar and sesame oil. Leave covered in the fridge until you are ready to make your dumplings.

Strain the stock, reserving the solids,* and check for seasoning. You may like to add an extra pinch of sea salt or sugar here, I know I do. Set the broth aside.

To make the dumplings, fill a small bowl with water (this is the water to dip your fingers in to seal the wrappers) and line a large tray with baking paper. Remove the wonton wrappers and prawns from the fridge and, with dry hands, remove the wrappers from their packaging. Working with one wrapper at a time, place one prawn in the centre, then dip your index finger in the water and dampen the edges of the wrapper. Gently lift one edge of your wrapper, folding it in half over the prawn to create a half-moon shape. Lightly press along the edges to seal, ensuring there are no gaps. Place the dumpling on the prepared tray, covering with a tea towel, and repeat until you run out of wrappers and filling.

Fill two large saucepans with water (one for the noodles and gai lan, the other for the dumplings) and bring them both to the boil. Separately, warm the broth over medium–high heat so that it is ready to be served. In one saucepan, cook the wonton noodles and gai lan for 45 seconds. Drain, running under cold water to remove any excess starch from the noodles, and set aside.

Carefully add the dumplings to the remaining saucepan of boiling water, cooking in batches if need be, and boil until they are translucent and you can see the prawn is bright orange and cooked through (about 2 minutes). Remove the dumplings with a slotted spoon and drain.

Divide the noodles, gai lan and wontons amongst your bowls. Ladle the hot broth over the top. Serve topped with the chopped spring onion and coriander and a drizzle of extra sesame oil.

Serves 6, with extra broth you can store in the freezer.

*Holy mother of food gods, *please please please* **do not** throw out your ham hock or your chicken once you have strained them. You can shred the chicken and use it to make a shredded chicken salad with julienned carrot and cucumber and sliced red onion and cabbage, mixed together with torn mint leaves, finely sliced chilli and peanuts. The dressing can be as simple as tablespoonfuls of honey, fish sauce and white wine vinegar mixed together. The ham hock can be transformed into a magnificent split pea and ham soup. I also add it to corn fritters like my mama used to make.

udon noodle soup

Admittedly, I've never had the patience to make my own noodles before, and always struggled to find a supermarket offering worth my while. That was until the Ginger and I discovered the brand Kama-age Udon in the freezer of our local Asian supermarket. Made in Japan, they are snap-frozen and are the closest I have come to enjoying restaurant-quality udon in my own home.

250 g udon noodles
Spring onion, finely diced, to serve
Wakame, to serve

Dashi broth

25 g kombu
20 g dried bonito flakes
4 tablespoons soy sauce
2 tablespoons mirin
1 teaspoon caster sugar
½ teaspoon sesame oil

For a dashi broth big enough for a portion to eat now and three to freeze for later, soak the kombu in a heavy-based saucepan filled with 2 litres of water for an hour, then slowly bring it to a simmer over medium heat. Remove the kombu. Add the dried bonito flakes to the water. Bring to the boil, then remove from the heat, allowing it to steep for 10 minutes before straining the broth through a fine sieve into another saucepan. Return the strained broth to medium heat, and add the soy sauce, mirin, sugar and sesame oil.

Cook the noodles according to the packet instructions. Ladle the dashi broth over your noodles in a soup bowl and serve with the spring onion and wakame.

Serves 2, with extra broth you can store in the freezer.

FEED

how to make
a filthy martini

I am not much of a fan of cocktails or spirits in general but my goodness, I really do love a vodka martini, especially when I am making one of my 'Single Lady Dinners'.

I have discovered that I prefer mine with truly excessive amounts of olive brine, which is why this is called a filthy martini. I also know that I must always stop at two!

15 ml olive brine
15 ml dry vermouth
60 ml vodka
Ice cubes
Sicilian olives, to garnish

Combine the brine, vermouth and vodka in a cocktail glass filled with ice. Stir all the ingredients briskly, then strain into a chilled martini glass. Garnish with as many olives as you'd like. I like to just drop mine in and fish them out with my fingertips, but you can put them on a toothpick too, if you prefer.

how to cook a steak
(with a salad for my sins)

I spent the four months I dated the Rower barbecuing a lot of meat. There are a few non-negotiables he taught me when it comes to cooking a steak, which I now swear by, because cooking a beautiful big piece of meat like this is a privilege, not an everyday convenience.

You will probably want to make sure that you have your exhaust fan on its highest setting and your smoke alarm temporarily removed to avoid setting off your apartment building's fire alarm and causing a mass evacuation and a potential $2000 fine, like I once did.

Along with the steak is my answer to the fact that I love vegetables but loathe salad. A flavourless bowl of leafy greens is such an immense disappointment to me. This is my delicious compromise, knobs of butter and all.

Steak

600 g rib eye steak, on the bone
Extra virgin olive oil
Sea salt flakes
Freshly ground black pepper
1 garlic clove, crushed with the palm of your hand
1 small French shallot (eschalot), finely chopped
1 sprig of thyme
1 tablespoon salted butter
1 teaspoon black peppercorns, coarsely crushed
1 tablespoon cognac
¼ cup thickened cream

Salad

2 tablespoons salted butter
2 garlic cloves, crushed
60 g frozen peas, thawed, or fresh snow peas, halved
120 g leafy greens
Sea salt and freshly ground black pepper
Zest and juice of 1 lemon

Before you start, make sure you bring your meat to room temperature, pat it dry, and season it generously by rubbing with a drizzle of olive oil and a big sprinkle of sea salt and black pepper. Make sure your cast-iron frypan is placed on high heat and piping hot (smoking even) before you begin—this helps with caramelisation and creates a deliciously crispy crust. When cooking, you want to aim to achieve a medium–rare result and can do so by cooking a 3 cm thick steak for 8 minutes. Cook it any further and your meat will be tough. To cook it evenly, you want to make sure you are turning it every 2 minutes. If your steak has a fat cap, use tongs to stand it on its side and cook for 3 minutes on each side.

Reduce the heat to medium–low. Add the garlic, shallot, thyme and butter and cook, basting the steak continuously for 2 minutes. Transfer the steak to a chopping board and leave your meat to rest for 5–10 minutes before slicing.

Meanwhile, to make your pepper sauce, add the crushed black peppercorns to the pan containing the garlic, shallot, thyme and butter, stirring until fragrant. Remove the pan from the heat and add the cognac, lighting with a lighter to evaporate. This often involves much shrieking and jumping around on my part: it is very exciting. Then add the thickened cream, return the pan to the heat and bring to a simmer to thicken the sauce.

For the salad, melt the butter in a large saucepan over low heat, add the garlic and stir until softened and fragrant. Stir through the peas or snow peas. Add the leafy greens and cook, stirring, until slightly wilted. Season with salt and pepper, add the lemon zest and juice, and stir through.

To serve, slice your steak against the grain (look for the parallel lines of muscle fibre that run down the meat, and slice perpendicular to them) and place on a serving plate. Return any juices from the steak to your sauce and stir them through, then pour the sauce over your sliced steak, with the sinful salad alongside. Season with a little more sea salt. I am a salt fiend after all.

the Ginger's dal with lemon rice

This is what the Ginger would make en masse and deliver to me so I would have something to heat and eat in the midst of writing this book. It is a recipe that is vegetarian and vegan and has completely transformed my perception (well, it was an absolute hatred) of lentils. We served it alongside lemon rice, which was also introduced to me by the Ginger. (The rice is also the perfect recipe to jazz up a store-bought lentil soup or to serve alongside steamed fish or grilled lamb.) The other thing we loved to serve this dal with was chapatti, which we attempted (and failed) to make at home. Instead we opted to buy the Katoomba-brand chapatti from the freezer section of our local supermarket or Indian grocer. We removed the flatbreads one by one from the freezer into the warm embrace of a dry non-stick frying pan, cooking them for 35 seconds on each side until golden brown. If you can't find toor dal, they are sometimes called pigeon peas, and chana dal is a good substitute. If you can't find the green chillies easily, you may be able to find the Katoomba brand in your local supermarket's freezer aisle.

Spice mix

1½ teaspoons red chilli powder
1 teaspoon ground turmeric
1½ teaspoons garam masala
1½ teaspoons dry mango powder
½ teaspoon asafoetida
2 teaspoons ground coriander

Dal

300 g toor dal, rinsed
1 teaspoon vegetable stock powder
3 bay leaves
½ teaspoon ground turmeric
80 g ghee
2 teaspoons cumin seeds
10 garlic cloves, crushed
2 large brown onions, finely diced
800 g tinned cherry tomatoes (I prefer Mutti brand)
2 cm piece of ginger, finely chopped
3 Indian green chillies, finely chopped
250 g baby spinach leaves
Sea salt flakes
Chapatti, to serve (optional)
Handful of coriander leaves, chopped, to serve

Lemon rice

1 cup jasmine rice
2 tablespoons ghee
2 teaspoons black mustard seeds
20 fresh curry leaves
4 cm piece of ginger, finely grated
1 teaspoon ground turmeric
Juice of 2 lemons

Combine all the spice mix ingredients in a bowl and stir. Set aside.

For the dal, place the rinsed toor dal in a bowl and cover with water to soak for an hour (it helps them to cook faster and taste better, too).

Drain the dal and add to a large pot alongside the vegetable stock, bay leaves, turmeric and 1.5 litres of tap water. Bring to the boil, and cook over medium heat for 20–30 minutes until the lentils are soft and easy to mush with the back of a wooden spoon. Remove from the heat, cover and set aside.

Heat the ghee in a large heavy-based cast-iron pot over medium heat. Add the cumin seeds, frying for a few seconds until fragrant. Add the garlic and onion and fry until golden.

Add the tomatoes, ginger and chilli and the spice mix to the pot, stirring until combined. Continue cooking over medium heat until the tomatoes are softened.

While the sauce is cooking, prepare the lemon rice. Cook the jasmine rice according to the packet instructions. Once it's ready, heat the ghee in a small frypan and add the black mustard seeds, curry leaves and ginger. Stir-fry for a minute or so and then delicately add the turmeric (that shit stains) and the lemon juice. Pour the mixture over your hot, cooked jasmine rice, and stir to combine. Set aside, with the lid on to keep it warm, while you finish the dal.

Once the tomatoes are softened, add the toor dal to the pot, including any remaining liquid it has cooked in. Then add the spinach, stirring to combine. Season with the sea salt flakes.

Serve the dal with the lemon rice and freshly fried chapatti and, if you like, garnish with the chopped coriander.

Serves 4.

Nanny's jam drops

One of my earliest memories of baking is with my nanny,
making jam drops together. To this day, whenever I beat
butter and sugar I still dip my finger into the mixture
to taste and, there in that morsel of batter, I find myself
sitting in Nanny's kitchen, my little legs swinging over
her countertop, licking the beaters of her old Kenwood
mixer clean. Nanny likes to say that I put more batter
into my mouth than the biscuits themselves.

250 g unsalted butter, softened

165 g caster sugar

1 teaspoon vanilla extract

2 free-range eggs

250 g self-raising flour, plus extra for rolling

1 jar fruit jam (raspberry, or your choice)

Preheat the oven to 175°C and line a baking tray with baking paper.

In the bowl of an electric mixer fitted with a paddle attachment, beat the butter, sugar and vanilla until nearly creamed. Add the eggs, one at a time, beating well after each addition. Add the flour and mix until a stiff dough forms. You may need to add a little extra flour here if the dough is too sticky in between your hands.

Cover your hands in more flour and roll the dough into small balls, about 30 g each. Place them on the baking tray leaving a 5 cm gap between each. Flatten the balls slightly and press your thumb into the middle of each biscuit to make an indent. Fill the hole with your jam of choice. I always choose raspberry but you could use fig, blueberry, strawberry or anything that tickles your fancy. Bake for 20 minutes or until golden.

banana bread/cake/ muffins

When I first moved into Commodore Street, I brought a box of freshly baked banana muffins to introduce myself to my new neighbours. I loved the beauty of bringing those spotted brown bananas back to life. This tried-and-tested recipe can be transformed into banana bread, banana cake, banana muffins or even a bundt cake with caramel sauce. Add nuts. Add chocolate. The choice is yours.

Unsalted butter, softened, for greasing
5 very ripe bananas, mashed
125 ml light olive oil
2 free-range eggs, at room temperature
1 free-range egg yolk, at room temperature
300 g brown sugar
1½ teaspoons vanilla bean paste
225 g self-raising flour

Preheat the oven to 180°C. Grease your chosen tin (loaf, muffin, bundt, 22 cm springform) with the butter.

Place the mashed banana, olive oil, eggs and egg yolk, brown sugar and vanilla in a mixing bowl and whisk to combine.

Gradually add the self-raising flour (being careful not to get too carried away like my mama) and mix to form your batter, which will be lumpy and thick, then pour it into your prepared tin.

Bake for 45 minutes to 1 hour, or until a skewer inserted in the centre comes out clean. Best eaten the same day, or toasted later with a generous dollop of butter. Lemon curd (or lemon butter, as my grandma used to call it to make it sound healthier) is also a delightful addition.

better-than-sex tiramisu

I have learned that tiramisu is a wonderful thing to eat instead of having mediocre sex. And I have also learned that tiramisu is the perfect dessert to plonk on the dining table with a handful of spoons at 3 am in the thick fog of a smoke machine, under the glow of a disco ball. Savoiardi have a beautiful way of soaking up not only coffee, but copious amounts of alcohol too.

6 free-range eggs
250 g caster sugar
2 teaspoons vanilla bean paste
1 kg Italian mascarpone, at room temperature
800 ml freshly brewed coffee, at room temperature
4 tablespoons coffee liqueur
800 g savoiardi biscuits (I prefer Balocco brand)
2 tablespoons Dutch-processed cocoa powder, sifted

Separate the eggs. Whisk the egg yolks, half the sugar and the vanilla bean paste in the bowl of an electric mixer on high until thick and pale and doubled in size (about 4–6 minutes). With the motor running, gradually add the mascarpone, one spoonful at a time.

In a separate mixing bowl, place half the egg whites. (You can freeze the remaining whites for future use.) Beat the egg whites until stiff peaks form. With the motor running, gradually add the remaining sugar, one spoonful at a time, until you have a shiny and stiff meringue.

Use a metal spoon to gently fold a third of the meringue into the mascarpone mixture, maintaining as much air as possible, then repeat in two more batches.

To layer the tiramisu, pick your preferred serving dish and spread a thin layer of the mascarpone meringue mixture on the base.

Combine the coffee and liqueur in a separate dish and, working patiently in batches, dip in your savoiardi, ensuring that each side of the biscuit has absorbed the liquid. (You want the biscuit to be soft but not falling apart.)

Arrange the biscuits, ensuring all the mascarpone is covered, then spread over half the remaining mascarpone mixture. Repeat with another batch of soaked biscuits and the remaining mascarpone. Add a final layer of lightly soaked savoiardi, cover in foil and leave in the fridge overnight. The next morning, use a fine sieve to dust the top of the tiramisu with the cocoa powder before serving.

chocolate olive oil cake

This was the very first cake I baked when I discovered that the Ginger's housemate was gluten and dairy intolerant. Baking with olive oil brings an incredible moistness you don't seem to get with butter.

150 g almond meal
½ teaspoon bicarb soda
50 g cocoa powder, plus extra for dusting
Pinch of sea salt flakes
150 ml extra virgin olive oil
200 g caster sugar
3 large free-range eggs, at room temperature
1 tablespoon vanilla bean paste
Double cream, to serve
Black sea salt flakes, to serve (optional)

Preheat the oven to 170°C. Grease a 20 cm springform cake tin with olive oil and line the base with baking paper.

In a bowl, combine the almond meal, bicarb soda, cocoa powder and sea salt, ensuring there are no lumps. Set aside.

Add the olive oil, sugar, eggs and vanilla to the bowl of your electric mixer fitted with a whisk attachment and whisk on high speed for 3 minutes, or until the mixture is pale and resembles thickened cream. Add the dry ingredients and whisk on low speed until just combined.

Pour the batter into the tin and bake for 40–45 minutes or until a skewer inserted in the middle of the cake comes out clean.

Allow it to cool completely in the tin before transferring to a cake stand. Dust with extra cocoa powder and serve with high-quality double cream, and some black sea salt flakes, if you like. Store leftovers in an airtight container at room temperature for 2–3 days.

double chocolate brownies, for the Ginger

I became enamoured with Laurie Colwin when I read in *More Home Cooking* that she felt 'it often seems the world divides (evenly or unevenly) into those who are waiting for dessert and those who have to produce it'. I always thought I was the person who was producing it, but now I really know I have been the one waiting for it, and rediscovering myself was the sweetest dessert of all.

When we first began to date, I remember the Ginger telling me that he would often finish twelve-hour days shooting weddings and then come home and have to figure out dinner for himself. I remember thinking that I wanted to cook for him, to care for him—to have dinner prepared for him. It's one of the first things I said to him after I told him I loved him. And as hard as that was to follow through on, given that we lived in separate houses, I was able to make him brownies each and every week.

Amelia said she thought the brownies would be the Ginger's and my 'thing'. 'Like Ina and Jeffrey,' she told me. 'Finally someone who appreciates and celebrates you.' She told me that Ina Garten and her husband Jeffrey have been together for over fifty years and that Ina's decadent brownie recipe is the essential ingredient in their long-lasting love because, as Ina says, the way to a man's heart is through his stomach. At sixteen years old, Ina would send a big box of brownies to Jeffrey at college, just like I would send the Ginger each week.

300 g caster sugar
80 g cocoa powder
150 g plain flour
1 teaspoon baking powder
250 g salted butter, melted
3 large free-range eggs, at room temperature
1 teaspoon vanilla bean paste
Pinch of sea salt flakes
180 g 70% dark cooking chocolate, roughly chopped

Preheat the oven to 160°C. Line a square baking tin with baking paper. (You can also make this recipe in a round springform cake tin or rectangular brownie tin, or even as individual brownie muffins or cupcakes.)

In a mixing bowl, combine the sugar, cocoa powder, plain flour, baking powder and melted butter. Add the eggs, vanilla and salt, whisking by hand until combined. Stir in the chocolate. Pour the batter into the tin and bake for 40 minutes. The batter will still be a little wobbly and a skewer won't be clean when you insert it because of the chopped chocolate, but trust that it will harden as it cools.

These brownies are best served warm with vanilla bean ice cream. You can keep them stored in an airtight container for up to a week. To serve, place a piece of brownie in the microwave and heat for no more than 30 seconds. What results is a deliciously warming chocolate pudding that stole the Ginger's heart.

burnt Basque cheesecake

I cannot stop baking this cheesecake. It's a cake so good it will make you cry. A cake that is impossible to stuff up because it's a cake that wants nothing more than to be burnt and blistered, cracked and crinkled, and yet still comes through in a cloud of captivating creaminess. A cake that is so perfectly imperfect, I long to bake it again and again and again because life is like that—perfect in all of its imperfections.

1 kg cream cheese, at room temperature
300 g caster sugar
6 free range eggs, at room temperature
500 ml thickened cream
2 teaspoons vanilla bean paste
80 g plain flour

Line a 20 cm springform cake tin with baking paper. There is no art or precision to this, I simply tear two sheets of paper and crisscross them so the paper extends above the height of your chosen tin.

Preheat the oven to 200°C. Beat the cream cheese and sugar in the bowl of an electric mixer fitted with a whisk attachment until smooth. Add the eggs, one at a time, whisking after each addition to combine. With a large spatula, scrape down the side of the bowl before adding the cream and vanilla and mixing to combine. Scrape down the side of the bowl once more, add the flour and mix to create a silky smooth batter. Pour into your tin and bake for 65–70 minutes, until you see the cheesecake's deliciously darkened top.

Remove from the oven. The cake will still wobble as though it is undercooked, but as it cools it will harden. Leave it in the tin for 10 minutes before removing it to cool completely. Serve at room temperature, on its own. This cake does not need a single thing added to it.

how to sabre champagne

The Ginger taught me to sabre champagne for the very first time. It's a life skill I never knew I needed, and now I am so excited to be able to share it within the pages of this book.

There are a few key things to note.

DO NOT sabre champagne aimed in the direction of anyone or anything you love.

Once the champagne is sabred, DO NOT clasp the now-jagged lip of the bottle with your hand. DO NOT put your mouth over the bottle to stop the champagne bubbles flowing. Yes, people have done that (including me) and, yes, there will be blood and, yes, it does hurt.

DO make sure your bottle has been chilling for at least three hours. DO make sure you keep your hand or finger holding onto the cork until the second you are ready to sabre. DO sabre with confidence. DO by all means treat yourself to a brand of champagne that typically shouldn't be wasted. This is your chance to be a Bougie Asshole like me.

DO tip the bottle upright immediately after sabring to avoid excess spillage.

First things first, you will need to retrieve a large knife from your kitchen. Next, you need to remove all foil from

FEED

the neck of the bottle, as well as its wire cage and the metal top, so everything's nice and smooth. As I said, make sure you keep your thumb or hand on top of the cork until the moment you are ready to sabre. Because of the pressure in the bottle, that freed cork will be ready and raring to go and there have been many moments (including the moment I was celebrating signing the contract for this little book) where that cork has popped prematurely.

Hold the bottom of the bottle in one hand at a 45-degree angle, aimed away from anything breakable—living or inanimate. With your other hand, hold the knife flat against the bottle, with the blunt edge facing the cork. Bring the knife slowly back towards you then quickly, firmly and with confidence thrust the knife along the glass of the bottle up to the cork. Once you have recovered from the surprise and delight of completing your first sabring, make sure to bring the bottle upright to avoid losing any precious liquid. Serve, sip and celebrate.

Celebrate life, celebrate one another, celebrate yourself.

acknowledgements

In writing this book I have been gifted with people's time and their memories of moments that have helped to shape me. There have been moments when they have retold a story from my life, and I have been so absorbed by the person in front of me and everything that's being said, that I have felt like it is the first time I am hearing it, the first time I am experiencing it. They would tell me of moments that were so outrageous, so deliciously wicked, that at the recollection of what we did, a deep belly laugh would roll from them and into me, and we would laugh till we lost our breath. And some of them would gently remind me of moments that wounded, when acid words and actions so harsh had made me silently whimper, made me cry. And then there were those times where our conversations collided and mingled as we spoke of our playful imaginings, when we dared to consider the impossible and planned for the possible—a memoir titled *Heartbake*.

Hannah Rose Yee, thank you for commissioning the essay, first published in *Vogue* Australia, on which this book is based. You are the spark that started the fire.

Grace Heifetz, who championed me and my words when they were nothing more than half-baked ideas fuelled by filthy martinis and tortellini. Thank you. I couldn't have done this without you.

Kelly Fagan, thank you for treating me as the writer you knew me to be, and waiting patiently until I became one. Your shared vision and belief in this book and your unwavering belief in me have been some of the most extraordinary things to have ever happened to me. Your friendship is the icing on the cake.

Ali Lavau, thank you for the gift of your brilliant brain, for helping me to knead my words till they formed something whole and for reminding me to show, don't tell.

To my heartbakers—phenomenal photographer Therese Bourne, food whisperer Kirsten Jenkins and right-hand woman Emma 'Guapa' Warren—thank you, from the bottom of my heart. Those three days shooting my recipes with you were some of the most nourishing, enriching, heart-expanding days of my life and this book is what it is because of you, and our shared heartache. Just remember: *the nose knows*. And to Louise Cooney: you welcomed us into the heartspace that is your home so we could create our recipes for *Heartbake*; I am so grateful and I cannot wait to cook for you.

Fran Haysey, I am blessed to have been gifted with your generosity, mind-blowing creativity and heart-bursting enthusiasm.

Louisa Maggio, thank you for deep-diving into our aspiring designer brains and bringing Kelly's and my eggish design to life. Justin Wolfers, thank you for expertly editing my recipes and allowing me to include an excessive use of salt in each. And Samantha Kent, Greer Gamble and Megan Johnston, thank you for curbing my excessive use of a comma, and for treating my words with such care.

My heartfelt thanks to every single person at Allen & Unwin who has worked to make this dream a reality. Especially Samantha Mansell, Sarah Barrett, Lou Playfair, Tom Gilliatt, Robert Gorman, Angela Handley, Peri Wilson, Rosie Scanlan, Matt Hoy, Andrew Cattanach and Ashleigh Jordan.

To my colleagues for their continued support, especially Tracey Cheetham, Mary Small, Praveen Naidoo, Maria Fassoulas and Ross Gibb. Thank you.

David Lovett, my friend and focaccia fanatic. Thank you for sharing your recipe with me. It is absolute perfection.

To my friends who not only lived through these stories but have allowed me to share them, who believed in me even when I didn't, thank you. I am indebted to Georgia O'Connor, Harrie Blundell, Chrystel Samson, Gabriela Palestra-Depasse, Nadine Ingram, Rob Kennard, Jyle Frame and Carl Pronti. And to Ken Blood and Kirsty Gibson, who welcomed me so warmly into their home, a place where so much of this book was thought about and subsequently written, and where a piece of my heart remains.

Ali Hammond, thank you for being my first reader and middle-of-the-sleepless-night messenger.

Amelia Brown, you've been the best thing waiting for me on the other side of each and every heartache. Thank you for making my heart so full.

To my grandparents and great-grandparents, for the many memories I have surrounding each and every single one of them, especially all the shared food memories. But most significantly, to my grampy. You are the most magnificent man, and I hope one day to meet another who loves me just as much as you do.

Jason and Natasha, thank you for making me proud to be a Ree.

Mama and Pa, thank you for your unconditional love. This book is as much yours as it is mine.

Miranda Vidal, Marilyn Tucker and Carly Tucker, thank you for making me feel so very welcome and so very loved.

Tarlan, Kaspar, Jonah and Jac—rediscovering you this past year has brought me overwhelming amounts of joy. I am so grateful for each and every one of you, and to our curdled, colourful family.

Diego Vidal, thank you for being my first love.

Dane Tucker, thank you for a year of magical thinking.

Margaret Condonis, thank you for helping me uncover the little girl who lingers within, longing to be seen and to be loved. *Hello, Little One. I see you. I love you.*

And most of all, my thanks to you, dear reader. I wrote *Heartbake* for me, but mostly for you.

Charlotte Ree lives in Sydney, Australia.
Heartbake is her second book.